Dirt *from* The New Yinzer.

Address correspondence, unsolicited material, subscription orders, and other queries to The New Yinzer, e-mail: info@newyinzer.com; Internet: www.newyinzer.com. Manuscripts and submissions will not be returned unless accompanied by a self-addressed, stamped envelope. Submission guidelines are available online, and electronic submissions are preferred.

 This project was made possible through the Pennsylvania Partners in the Arts program of the Pennsylvania Council on the Arts (PCA), a state agency. It is funded by the citizens of Pennsylvania through an annual legislative appropriation, and administered locally by ProArts. The PCA is supported by the National Endowment for the Arts, a federal agency.

Printed and bound in the USA in an edition of 2,000 copies.

ISBN 0-9748532-1-6   *First Printing*

Book designed by Brett Yasko.

Contents.

THE NEW YINZER

Jennifer Meccariello, *EDITOR*

EDITORIAL BOARD
Dave Griffith
Eric Lidji
Seth Madej

BOOK DESIGN
Brett Yasko

www.newyinzer.com

About this book.

This book digs into a non-literal interpretation of "dirt"–what we hide, what we sweep away, what we wallow in, and what we cover up. We asked writers to surprise us with their bleak honesty discussing something they're not supposed to. Could they tell us a secret they had never told before? Could they transform the sensational into a compelling story?

They could.

We weren't looking for pieces that exposed real people's secrets without their permission, nor were we looking for the quintessentially maudlin. *Dirt* is a place to explore what's hiding under the couch, shut tight in the upstairs cupboard, and locked away in the dark parts of a person, place, or thing. It's fourteen dirty little secrets straight from us to you.

Lean close and listen.

Dirt is funded by a generous grant from the Pennsylvania Partners in the Arts program of the Pennsylvania Council on the Arts.

Dirt.

Sherrie Flick's I Call This Flirting *(Flume Press, University of California, Chico) won the 2003-04 Fiction Chapbook Award. Her stories have appeared in numerous literary journals including* North American Review, Prairie Schooner, Quarterly West, New Orleans Review, *and* Puerto Del Sol. *She has received fellowships from the Ucross Foundation and Atlantic Center for the Arts, and an Artist Opportunity grant from ProArts, Pittsburgh. She is the director of the Gist Street reading series and lives in Pittsburgh.*

Lenny the Suit Man

BY SHERRIE FLICK

Lenny comes upstairs to our offices about once or twice
a month. His van is idling in the back parking lot: The
Suit Van. With his tape measure, he crawls all over us
at our desks. Phones ring. I'm trying to photocopy.

Frank says, "Lenny. Come off it. We got suits,
see? We don't need any more."

But Lenny has this way with people. He doesn't
give up. His suits are nice and cheap. I'm moping in
the corner, telling myself I'm not thinking about
Veronica, even though I'm scratching "V," "V," "V"
along the border of my desktop planner. I go down
with the other guys. Lenny flicks his tape measure,
trots ahead of us even though he knows our measurements by heart. That's why we like him—he's effi-
cient, does his job, treats us right.

The suits aren't hot; he swears it, and you've got to
believe him. There's something about his face. It tells
you, *Hey. I've known pain. I don't need to steal suits.*

That's what it tells me, anyway. I'm Bob, and I believe in Lenny.

Lenny chatters about fabric colors matching flecks in the eyes and about quality—how it doesn't come knocking on your door every day. That's a joke. Lenny pauses, and when we laugh, he laughs too—a big chuckle for such a little man, which makes us laugh more. Lenny makes us happy even when the guys from upstate are making us crunch numbers, looking for another budget cut.

In his van, there's an espresso machine bolted to a piece of wood. He sets it on the driver's seat after parking. It runs off the cigarette lighter. I ask him why he doesn't get a Mr. Coffee, tell him it would at least squirt out a decent amount. We stand around looking at suits, sipping espresso out of big white Styrofoam cups. Lenny insists, tells us it's classy and European, tells us we need class in order for his suits to reach their full potential. He apologizes for the cups, says he wants china, but his cousin Sandy got a deal on five cases of twelve-ounce Styrofoam. Lenny says, Sandy says no china until the cups are gone. Sandy's an investor, so whatever he says goes.

I order a brown suit. I need it. Lenny says he'll bring it back in a couple of weeks, ready to fit my body like a glove should fit a hand.

The air is cool and crisp. The sky, bright blue. Everything anticipates the winter that's coming after this fall. I'm not ready for winter or anything that frozen and unstoppable. Yesterday, when it was raining like hell, I was the weather. Me. Right there, present tense. I didn't even use my umbrella—walked the whole way home in my dark blue single-breasted with nobody looking twice. Now the cold I don't deserve has started in. The brown suit is mine.

I haven't told Lenny about my smashed-up heart or let on about how Veronica yanked it out and tossed it down two flights of stairs. But he knows something is wrong. I should be jabbing him more about his coffee instead of just sitting here, sipping it quietly, like some European guy who drinks this stuff every day with his ankles crossed, pinkie raised.

I would like to mention pity. Pity. I hate it. It's those moist puppy eyes people throw at you like they have any idea what you're going through. Like they know what she said as she slammed the door and headed down the two flights of stairs from my apartment. Stomping, mind you, on my squishy throbbing heart with each step—two harder stomps on the landing between the floors.

She said, "Bob. I don't date stupid guys."

I spent the last two nights listening to old country music. It's what I do under duress. The Patsy Cline tape is store-bought and squealing that high-pitched-ready-to-go-at-any-moment alarm this morning while I was in the shower. After work, I'm buying a new one.

Lenny sees right through it all—pulls me aside and says, "Fuck her. I can see that so-sad look on you, Bob. Don't let her get the best of you. Your measurements will change. I've seen it a million times."

I nod in Lenny's direction, swallowing hard. This whole interaction is so close to ominous, goose bumps dot my arms; tears are brimming in public. I can't believe it. As Lenny hugs me, all my co-workers turn in unison to watch. This is the beginning of my problems. They end with Susan, but that's another story completely. I know my life is going to collapse before it puffs up. I'm certain my heart will never fit right again.

I ask to try on another suit and say, "Lenny. I'm not a stupid guy."

Lenny says, "No, Bob. No way," like he's trying to drive a point home—he looks at me like we have an inside joke about this. Lenny does not pity me or pat me on the shoulder, which is why I don't appreciate it when Frank walks up and does just that.

Three or four pats and Frank says, "You okay, Bob? Got what you want?"

In retrospect, I realize, I took this all wrong. *Pity*, I think. *I hate it.* I think, *Hell no. I am not okay. I did not want Veronica stomping down my stairs wearing my favorite flannel shirt I'd loaned her because she was cold.*

So I whisper, "Frank, just fuck off."

This doesn't go over well. Frank is my boss and soon, without much wind-up, he's like I've never seen him. He's jogging back and forth with his fists curled and shoulders hunched. The van is rocking, and he's throwing punches in my direction. He's sputtering something like, "Yeah. *Comeatme*. Yeah. *Comeatme*." Espresso spills onto the white-linen double-breasted Stan just ordered for his spring vacation. I'm ducking and swallowing hard with my own fists feebly clenched in front of my face the way Father Vincent showed me the afternoon after Billy Wenning smeared me across the Sacred Heart playground. I can taste the brine in my throat. Lenny is the only one staying calm. Soon he's the only one staying in the van. All my co-workers rush out onto the sidewalk.

Lenny says, "Frank. Frank." Real steady, like he's done it a million times. Suit jackets are flying as Frank's in full force. Lenny methodically taps Frank on the forehead—somehow finding his forehead amongst the flurry of punches he's throwing mostly into the air—with a soft thudding noise.

Frank slows as his fists make larger and larger windmills; his legs stop dancing, and he collapses onto the orange shag carpet mumbling something like, "Lint." He rubs his face back and forth across the worn scratchy stubble that I imagine must smell like St. Bernard.

I run out of the van, past my huddled and whispering co-workers, and across the parking lot—bent over on the verge of dry heaves. After a while, I pull a handkerchief carefully out of my back pocket and blow my nose. I grab the box of Tic-Tacs out of my breast pocket.

Back in the van, Frank is slowly standing up and Lenny is out mumbling to my co-workers who seem— from my point of view—more interested in my heaves than the thousands of punches their boss just managed to throw. Frank didn't hit me once. He flogged a lot of hanging suits and, as I mentioned, the air; but he never touched me.

Lenny walks across the asphalt lot, puts his hands in his pockets, looking optimistic. He says, "Frank wouldn't hurt you, Bob. He's just under a lot of pressure these days. Downsizing. You understand. The brown suit's on me when it comes in. Totally free of charge."

Frank slinks over with apologies, talking softly about deadlines and a sick German shepherd at home. I nod my head, shuffle my feet, shrug, saying, "No harm done." Frank walks back into our building. Later he'll take me out for a beer.

Lenny looks off into the distance beyond his idling van toward the flat horizon and the plaza malls, antsy to get going. I say, "Hey man, thanks for doing that forehead thing. You probably saved my life."

Lenny shrugs, says, "Tai chi."

I shake his hand. I don't like hugging guys.

The next month I'm at a party I don't want to be at, but my co-workers were starting in on the "being a hermit all my life" deal. I pour myself a nice drink: short glass, ice, vodka. No fruit. Most people hate this, but I think it looks clean. Nothing like a nice clean drink. I'm sipping my vodka, looking over Joe's shoulder while he's beating Frank at cribbage. He's kicking Frank's ass, and I'm enjoying myself immensely because nobody feels the need to talk to me or check on me or anything. Joe really wants a promotion, but I know he's not getting one, so I'm happy he's at least getting some satisfaction. And then, wham. There she is: Veronica. She's at the one party I decide to attend in the four weeks since she ruined me. Of the vast array of parties that must be going on, Veronica is looking across the room, squinting at me, and waving hi like I'm not a stupid guy at all, but a casual acquaintance whose name she just can't place right now but knows she should be polite to. She smiles. Someone takes her coat, which means she's staying.

I'm not even nervous that I'm about to have a breakdown standing on Bill and Francis' pristine eggshell carpet. They're very nice people in a seemingly healthy relationship, and they served shrimp cocktail specifically because it's my favorite. I wave back politely. I notice—and I may be wrong—the whole room stop, take a collective sigh, then kick in with their idle chatter again.

I think, *Yes, I see. Veronica and I are now the kind of people who wave across rooms.*

Veronica is pleased with this transaction and nods like she would to an obedient dog. She heads toward the kitchen or maybe the bathroom. I don't know because I beeline it to the back door, sit on the steps

smoking the pack of cigarettes I palmed from the coffee table on my way out. They're British or French
or Canadian, shorter than American cigarettes and
tasty. I feel pretentious smoking them, which is a
good thing because pretentious is a hell of a lot better than pathetic.

Soon I pick out Veronica's laugh in the living
room. I can see her beautiful, naked body standing
by the coffeemaker in my kitchen as she quietly tells
me that as soon as she's had her coffee, she's going
to take me down. Right there on the ceramic floor.
She says, "I want *you*," whispers quietly, "Only *you*."

The thing is, Veronica didn't want *me*. She wanted
him. And it has to do with more than pronouns. To
be specific, she wanted David. The very next day.
These details get around, then they get back to me.
For this, I'm thrilled. Veronica wants David. I'm a
stupid guy.

Yes. I know. I'm damaged goods for a long time to
come. I'm wrapped in plastic and taped at weird angles.

I finish my fancy cigarette and start walking home,
even though Joe's expecting a ride to try and keep me
at the party longer. I walk home—what must be five
miles—kicking stones and putting my hands in my
front pockets like it's a sad movie, and I'm the star.

Down side streets, across some alleys, and then I'm on the main drag. A few dark storefronts: a dry cleaner, a Laundromat, a Sicilian pizza joint that never seems to be open. The whole world feels like a ghost town now except for the All-Nite Diner. I stumble past the shadow of its neon glow. That's where Susan is—the part of the story I won't get to. There's Susan, and my future, with her green eyes, her lazy blink, that wry smile. She's inside, ready, while I'm on the sidewalk shuffling through my gloom. I'm thinking about Veronica, about the coat I gave her, the flannel shirt, the smell of coffee, her legs and lips.

By the time I get home, I'm feeling like the useless punk my mother assured me I'd turn out to be. My feet hurt. I take off my socks and shoes and pour some vodka into my favorite glass, the old one that says Idaho. Beside a state map are two skiers who look the way I suppose they thought love looked back in the 1950s. They're curvy but muscle-less as they smile and point toward the potato state with confidence. The woman rests her head on the man's shoulder, content like they have a lovely suburban home and two kids back in Wichita, Kansas. I fill the glass up to their ankles.

As I fiddle with the radio tuner, trying to get reception for a jazz or classic rock station, it comes to me. I need a suit. It's a craving. Suddenly, I need one—hunter green, with slightly wider lapels than the brown one. A suit I'll look good in even with the jacket unbuttoned. A new attitude isn't coming any time soon, but the suit is just a phone call away. I pour more vodka, no ice—to the knees.

I call Lenny, turn off the saxophone solo coming from the radio and put on Hank Williams. The phone rings eight times before Lenny picks up. It's been two weeks since he dropped off the brown suit. When he answers, he sounds groggy, but I start in on how much I appreciate my brown suit. How I wore it yesterday and got compliments on the way it accented my shoulders.

"Lenny, you're amazing. I understand what you're getting at. I really do. Suits, man. Suits, Lenny. Lenny, I love you, man."

Halfway through this last sentence I realize I'm more than likely more than half drunk, but the words keep coming and I'm not so much concentrating now on what they are as not slurring them as they come out.

"Lenny," I say, "I need a suit. Hunter green, man, hunter green."

He says, "Just a minute there, Bob. Bob? Just a minute," and he cups his hand over the receiver. This green suit has become important. I know I can never make it clear enough to Lenny.

Eventually he says, "You been drinking, Bob?"

I say, "Yes, Lenny. Yes, I have. Vodka, no ice, man. No ice."

He says, "Good. Good. I'll be over. You said green, right?"

"Right. Hunter green. Wide lapels. It's the color, man. Green. It'll change my life."

Lenny says, "Bob, you see her tonight?"

"Yes, Lenny. She had on the coat I gave her for her birthday."

"Okay, Bob, okay then. You gave her a coat?"

"Yeah. Part of the reason why I'm stupid."

Eventually I give him my address, and we hang up.

The next thing I know I'm face down in my own shag carpet, which does—for some reason—smell like dog. Lenny rolls me over, sits me in my chair and rummages through my drawers. I'm wondering how he got into my house, suspecting those suits might have stories to tell.

I say, "Hey, Lenny. What're you looking for in all those cupboards there?"

He says, "Coffee filters. And they're drawers. Those are cupboards. I already looked in there."

"Don't have any."

"No coffee filters?"

"No coffee. No filters. No machine. Tossed 'em. I'm supposed to be starting this wheat-free, caffeine-free, soy milk protein-based thing. My sister's idea. She reads a lot of magazines."

Lenny holds up a plastic sack of brown rice flour. "This isn't going to work."

Lenny has on a T-shirt and jeans. He looks good. European. His hair is slicked back the way I've always wanted to do mine.

He says, "You'll definitely need coffee if you're going to get measured for this thing." He motions toward the couch and the suit splayed across it is the perfect shade of green. At that moment I realize I need to take things more seriously. Lenny is a symbol, a role model, a mentor. I'm overcome with emotion, crying turns into big heaping sobs.

Lenny busies himself with washing my dishes. The dull clink of glasses in suds makes me feel better. I'm ready to stand up; I reach for the box of Kleenex as Lenny carefully stacks my plates and bowls in the drying rack.

He says, "All ready to go, Bob?"

I follow him out my door and into the crisp late

night. At the bottom of my driveway the Suit Van is waiting, the streetlight shines off Lenny's logo, a jacket on a hanger with wheels at the bottom.

We drive toward Eighth Street with the windows down, cool air rushing in. I can smell earth and road and night. Every so often, I think I hear Veronica's laugh, off in the distance, beyond the rows of darkened houses and swaying pines. But I know that's just my head. We drive by the All-Nite Diner where I see the door gliding shut. Next week I'll stop in for a cup of coffee, a slice of pie. I'll look up and notice Susan writing out the Specials Board.

Lenny parks at a lookout point I've never known about, shifts order forms around and plugs in the espresso maker. He messes with the coffee and then sits back in the creaky faux-leather seat, lets out a big sigh.

"Smoke?" he says.

I say, "No. No. Gave it up a few hours ago."

Lenny nods. Finally, the coffee gurgles into its little metal pot. Lenny says, "I'm getting china next week."

I sit staring at the twinkling town I live in thinking every single person understands how to make progress in this world, except me. I say, "That's really great, Lenny."

I swirl my coffee around in the oversized Styrofoam cup and try to think seriously about my life, but get distracted instead. I line events up in my head so they make sense, and they jiggle themselves into hexagons and triangles. I say, "Lenny. You know, I think I'd be okay if I just didn't expect so much or want so much decency in this world, so much fairness."

Lenny doesn't answer. Just nods. Eventually he starts up the van and says, "We've still got to get you fitted, and there's the birds starting up."

On the way home we talk baseball scores, fishing holes, Frank and those swinging punches.

As the sun rises, Lenny is serious, crawling around on my floor with straight pins propped in his mouth, his tape measure snaking along behind. He's immaculately pressed—the perfect salesman—as he slides the green jacket over my arms, tugs on a pant leg, stands back to see if I look good, then begins again.

Michael Byers is the author of The Coast of Good Intentions, *a book of stories, and* Long for This World, *a novel. He teaches fiction at the University of Pittsburgh.*

Wynn's Story

BY MICHAEL BYERS

When they were very young Wynn's parents had
eloped and been married in Idaho, an event they dis-
cussed with such rigorous absence of sentiment he
suspected they were in fact desperate romantics and
would not admit to it for fear of seeming, in this cyn-
ical age, ridiculous. They had been just twenty. The
marriage had lasted long enough to produce Wynn
and to create, upon its dissolution, a furious anger on
the part of his mother and a fond, wistful bafflement
on the part of his father. Wynn resembled his father
in most ways and particularly in matters of love, apt
to escort bees from the room in a cup and liable, especially in his younger days, to profess undying de-
votion at the drop of a hat. This tendency moderated
as he grew older and his own marriage was a model
of affection and passion, and as a man he was proud
of the life he had built for himself. His parents had
each remarried and for some years he did not have
to worry about what was happening with them. His
father moved to Baltimore and his mother sold her

house and moved to a houseboat. Eventually his father grew sick and began to die. He was a short stocky man with a white mustache and a wild head of elderly hair, an affectation, as in his working life he had been conservative in dress and manner. Against the pillow his hair was a tangle. "Who do I look like?" his father asked.

"Einstein."

"Exactly! That's what an old man should look like. Should look like a damn-it-all-to-hell," said his father. His father's second wife was there, Juliette, a woman twenty years younger but as passionate, and as capable of fury, as Wynn's mother. His father had exchanged women but had not strayed far from his original intent. Juliette knew this, Wynn suspected, and in Wynn's presence anyway she behaved with the self-conscious directness of an understudy. Baltimore was not Wynn's favorite city in the world but his father's gravestone would not be there, it would be back in Kansas City, where his father had been born unimaginably long ago. It turned out to be a nice stone, black and polished, standing on a little hill in a way that reminded Wynn of his father himself, the way he had seen the man as a child, very tall and dark and stern and slender, unbreakable.

Now he had broken. His mother across the country was almost senile by then, but she knew the name. "That bastard," she told him. Her houseboat needed maintenance but Wynn could not afford to pay and neither could she, and there was a sickening list in the living room that caused the furniture to slide. "You know what he's all about. He's all about sex. S-E-X!"

"He's dead, ma," Wynn said.

"Dead, dead, dead, whatever. That's what it was all about! That whole trip! That whole experience of my life!"

His mother died soon thereafter and Wynn scattered her ashes off the end of her pier. She had had a good time living on the lake and he liked the idea of her living there forever in some way. He inherited the houseboat and eventually saved enough money to keep it afloat and upright. Evenings on the lake were particularly nice, the lights of the city sloped up from the water and the seaplanes when they landed feathered the air. He and his wife in their own retirement spent a number of nights there, though the acoustics of the place were peculiar and beneath their heads the water knocked around the pontoon with a hollow slap. It had been a long drive to Idaho in the old days, he knew; it would have taken his parents a day at least to get there. He struggled to imagine it. Why had they had done it? What animal surge of passion could have taken them that far, eloping in silence on those terrible roads? And what would his children say about him? What would he be remembered for? What moment would they choose and say, This was my father, can you imagine doing this, can you imagine such a thing, oh! what a strange and marvelous man he must have been?

Melissa Altenderfer's work has appeared in Yawp, The Taproot Literary Review, Pittsburgh City Paper, Ms., Water~Stone, *and in the anthology* September 11, 2001: American Writers Respond, *edited by William Heyen. She is the Public Reading Series Coordinator for the International Poetry Forum in Pittsburgh, where she lives with her retired racing greyhound, Penny.*

Greiving Son Shrink-Wraps Mom's Body

—The Weekly World News

Who do you tell when somebody dies?
She was the one who knew how to talk
all nice with the guys who came to take
away our furniture sometimes, the wound-
up landlady when the rent check bounced,
the government people who tried to cut
my disability payments. All the twisted

complicated stuff. Not that I just laid
around. I knew how to use the vacuum
and separate the laundry. I mowed
the lawn, did the garbage. She showed
me how to preserve tomatoes from our
garden in jars. I lifted them from the boiling
water when her arms got too weak. Seal
them with rubber rings and put them down
cellar, and they'll stay fresh as spring.

When things got too bad she'd open
up her jewelry box and sift through
for something good to sell. I looked
there after she'd gone, but the diamonds
and the fakes all looked the same to me.

It's like when I used to try to weed
the garden. She'd yell at me if I cracked
open a bug cocoon or some old brown
seed pod. You never know what's
going to come out of that, she'd say.
It could be something beautiful.

MELISSA ALTENDERFER

Kathleen E. Downey received a Masters degree in writing from Carnegie Mellon University. Her fiction and poetry have appeared in publications such as the Pittsburgh Quaterly, *the* Loyalhanna Review, Truce, Pendulum, *and* Pudding. *Her story "Everyone Needs a Door to Close" won the 2001 Taproot Literary Review award for fiction.*

Trust Exercise

BY KATHLEEN E. DOWNEY

My grandmother had eight children and like a string of beads, they all looked alike. Today, people talk about it as if she had eight heads. She might have felt as if she did. One day, when my father was eleven, my grandmother put a mincemeat pie into the oven, walked upstairs to the third story of the house, and threw herself out the front bedroom window. No one else was there, except my father who was sick with a virus. He apparently heard her rustling in the front bedroom, padded into the room behind her, and then watched her swing her legs out the window and press both hands against the ledge to push her buttocks away from the building.

He ran to the window and looked out to see his mother's head cocked to one side in the snow and her legs going in two different directions as if she were leaping in front of a stark, white curtain. He raced down three flights of stairs, stood over her in his bare feet, shook her, and then dashed a block to his aunt's house. He told his aunt exactly what had happened. His aunt jogged to his house in only an apron and housedress, with him trailing behind. She stood over her sister and ordered my father to go inside and to put on some clothing and shoes. She followed him, picked up the phone to call the police, noticed that the oven was on, put down the phone, and opened the oven door.

"Oh God help her!" she said. "A mincemeat pie! Why in the world was that the last thing she made?"

My grandmother had been an expert baker and had made ornate cakes for the most elite weddings in Pittsburgh. Mincemeat pie was an odd choice for her.

Later, my father's aunt told the policemen that her sister had fallen accidentally while she was washing the window. One of the policemen asked my father what he saw. He would not answer. Perhaps I've seen too many bad movies, but I don't know why the policemen wouldn't have questioned the window-washing story when there weren't any cleaning supplies near the window. Until I was fourteen, only my parents knew anything besides the stock window-washing story.

My parents fought loudly, often, and consistently throughout my childhood. All of their fights were about the same three topics: the house was not clean, dinner was not ready when my father got home from work, and there was no money. During one of their money fights, the seal that trapped my grandmother's secret burst.

My mother had bought a new dress for a wedding—a drapey, rose-colored chiffon confection with bell sleeves and an uneven hemline. She had left it hanging from the china closet in the dining room. She and I were alone in the kitchen when my father arrived home from work.

"What's that?" my father asked as he entered the house. He looked at the mail and shoved his car keys into the pocket of his brown water authority uniform while he waited for an answer.

"It's a dress," my mother said.

"I can see it's a dress, Helen. What's it doing here?"

"It's for the wedding Saturday."

"How much?"

"Larry!"

"How much, Helen?"

She refused to tell him.

"Take it back," he said.

"I will not!"

"We've got four children to feed. You've got a closet full of clothes. You're not spending any more of my money on a dress you're going to wear once.

Wear the dress you wore to church on Sunday, for Chrissake. And take that thing back!" he shouted.

"No!"

My father slammed the mail onto the table, marched to the dining room, and pulled the chiffon confection away from the china closet. We heard a loud, mournful shriek of hanger being pried from wood. He strode past my mother and out the door. She and I ran to the window.

"Back off, Bitsy," my mother snapped at me.

I stayed at the window and watched my father shove the dress into the trunk of his car. He marched back into the house, his legs like frantic scissor blades opening and closing. The screen door slammed.

"Now get the goddamned dinner on the table," he shouted. He picked up the mail again, pulled it apart, and held it close to his face.

I could tell that he wasn't reading each piece of mail—just taking a stance. And my mother wasn't going to stand for the stance. She went to his chair and snapped an envelope from his hand.

"You are crazy!" She put her face right against his. "You're crazy just like your goddamned crazy mother. No wonder she killed herself. *I'd* kill myself too if I had to raise you, you son of a bitch!"

My father threw the mail down, pushed back his chair and left the house. I heard his car start and speed away. The gravel in the alley protested. My mother sunk down in his chair and made circles on her forehead with her hands. She rubbed her eyes and fastened the points of her navy blue Keds on the linoleum. She sniffed and said in a wet, congested voice, "Suzanne, finish setting the table." My mother only called me by my given name, Suzanne, when she was angry. Ordinarily, I was always "Bitsy." When I was a baby I was so tiny that my aunt had called me her itsy-bitsy one. The Bitsy part stuck—and no one called me anything else.

I had already finished setting the table, but I didn't dare say anything. I straightened the silverware that was beside the plates. The timer on the oven sounded, but my mother did not move.

"I didn't know that Daddy's mother killed herself," I said as I shut off the timer.

My mother looked at me as if she would slap me. "*Shut your mouth* and set the table!" She ran her hands through her short, red, wiry hair, and then she looked up at me. "I'm sorry."

She had never said the words "I'm sorry" to me in my whole life, not even when she accidentally dropped the hot iron on my hand.

She got up from the chair, reached her tiny, pin-like arm across the counter, and fished for a cigarette and her lighter. "Your father's mother killed herself." She lit her cigarette and blew a hard puff of smoke toward the ground.

She told me the story—that my father had told her in detail years before—of my grandmother pitching herself from the window. She said that she forgave my father for his behavior because she knew that in everything he did there was the memory of that horrible day.

"I'd like to dig that bitch up and kill her again for what she did to him," she said and just when I was starting to think that her concern for my father was touching, she added, "Because she's sure made *my* life hell."

Then she told me that I could never, ever repeat that story to anyone—not to any family member or friend and not even to my future husband or children. And I was certainly never to bring it up to my father. He was not to know that she had told me. "It's a very shameful thing for your father. For everyone," she said. If anyone asked, I was to stick to the window-washing story. She made me promise and I did, but I never understood why it was a secret and why it was shameful. For almost two decades, until about a year after my father's death, I kept my promise, in the same way that I kept the charm bracelet my father had given me for my First Communion. I moved that bracelet from my parents' house to three different apartments, although I had worn it only twice during my childhood. Every so often, my father would ask, "Do you still have your First Communion bracelet?" and tell me that when I had a daughter I could give it to her. One day, my apartment was robbed and the bracelet was taken, along with all of the other jewelry that was in the same box. I didn't notice that it was gone until I moved again. Fortunately, my father never asked me about it after it was stolen.

I thought about my grandmother only on and off for the next few years. I almost let the secret of her death slip when my sister Maureen was home for Christmas during her first year of college. I was in twelfth grade and Maureen's semester away had enlarged her head enough to make her think she was much more sophisticated than I. We were in the dining room two days before Christmas with some of her high school friends. She talked about Chicago, where she had been a student for three-and-a-half months, as if she had lived on Lakeshore Drive all her life. After her friends left, as we brushed stray bits of popcorn from the table and stacked empty glasses, I tripped over a throw rug and slammed into the china closet. My sister scolded me—something about me almost smashing Great-Great Aunt Ida's priceless, antique teapot.

"I didn't know we *had* a Great-Great Aunt Ida," I said. "I thought Mom got that thing at Gold Circle."

I thought, even if we do have a Great-Great Aunt Ida, it's not like you've ever *met* her.

"There's a lot that *you* don't know," she sneered. "There were great artists and artisans in our family! But you wouldn't know that," she said. "You've never paid attention to family history like I have. You're lucky you know our grandparents' names." As I rubbed the fresh bruise on my arm, the story of my grandmother's death rose in my mind. I was the only one besides my parents who knew it. I thought, I could let her have it—stop her right there.

"I know plenty that you don't know," I said.

"Like what?" she cocked her head to one side. She had started wearing college-girl clothes and so much make-up. She had come back from Chicago looking like an adult. But at that moment, she looked the way she had in grade school, daring me to disobey our parents. Her affects of maturity faded away. I could hear my father shuffling around in the bedroom upstairs. My brush with the China closet had woken him. I thought he might come downstairs and yell, "Will you girls knock it off!"

"Never mind," I said.

When the secret finally did come out, I was working as a software quality assurance tester. I used the programs that the software engineers at my company built and then reported the defects so that they could be fixed before the customers found them. It meant telling people things about their work that weren't nice. I was entering data into the database one day when I stopped to read an e-mail from the software development director. It ordered everyone in the department to clear their calendars for the following Friday so that we could all attend a team-building seminar. Not thirty seconds later, Anita appeared at my desk. She was a quality tester like me, and we had worked together for ten years. If I admitted to having friends at work, then Anita was my best work friend. Anita and I didn't understand why companies wanted all their employees to get along and be friends.

We had friends. We were at work for a paycheck, not a social life. We didn't want to be *liked*. We wanted to be able to leave at five so that we could be with the people whom we had actually *chosen* as friends.

Anita peered over the wall of my cube, her blue eyes were like missiles and her red, wiry hair seemed to be wilder and higher than usual. She folded her spindly arms over her tiny, wafer-like body. She looked so angry, that her freckles seemed to be blinking.

"Did you see this bullshit about this bullshit all-day seminar?" she spat. "When am I supposed to do my goddamned work?"

"I guess you missed the last seminar about inappropriate language in the workplace?"

"If they keep us even one minute late, *they're* paying the fee to that daycare." She pounded her tiny index finger into the corner of my cube wall. "*Team*-building my ass! They want us to kiss the engineers' butts! They want us to say it's okay send us broken code and expect us to test it."

"Maybe they want the engineers to kiss our butts," I gave her a fake smile.

Anita and I agreed to sit together at the seminar so that if they divided us into pairs to do some stupid exercise, we would be each other's partners and we could talk about something else during the exercise.

Anita was already seated in the training room when I arrived early Friday morning. She had claimed the seat next to hers for me with a coffee mug.

"Oh *no*," she said. "Look who's headed this way."

Charles, one of the software engineers, walked to a chair on the other side of Anita. Charles was a devout member of some rare Christian denomination whose name I could never remember. He and his wife home-schooled their children and were involved almost daily with their church. A dark-brown crosshung in Charles' cubical and his screen saver said "Repent, for the kingdom of heaven is near." Anita did not like Charles.

"He has no right to bring that holy-roller shit into the office!" she said to me once. "It's separation of church and state. That's the law."

"We don't work for the state." I said. "And so what? It's a free country. He can be religious as long as he doesn't force us to be religious."

"He gives me the creeps. Did you see him get up and move at the status meeting when Andrew sat down beside him?"

"No."

"Don't you get it? Andrew's gay. Charles thinks gay people are going to hell."

"Oh he *does not*, Anita! He's a harmless little guy. He's not like you and me, but he's not *bothering* anyone. You're being silly."

"You're naïve. If we let people like him keep up what they're doing, they'll have us all attending mandatory chapel every morning before work. You know, he's never even seen an R-rated movie. He told me so. He's always got that smirk on his face. He thinks he's superior. Those people don't just *worship* God. They think they *are* God. He's pure evil!"

I usually felt like Anita and I were on the same path about most things, but I also secretly thought she was paranoid and that the real reason she didn't like Charles was because he gave her a hard time when she submitted software defects that he had to fix. He told her that she was too picky and returned most of her defect reports marked "by design"— meaning somehow the mistakes she found were *supposed* to be there.

Charles' family came to visit him at work one day. I saw them together in the parking lot. His wife was pregnant, quite a bit shorter than he, and her hair fell almost to her hips, like a cape around her shoulders. His boys wore matching shorts and shirts and had identical crew cuts. Charles held the little girl and when he attempted to hand her back to his wife, the child wailed. He took her back in his arms and rocked her until she was calm. How could Anita think that he was evil?

Charles put his notebook down next to Anita and pulled back the chair. He nodded to both of us. Anita grunted. I waved. I could see Anita pouting.

After all of the scheming Anita and I had done, the seminar instructor paired us off so that Charles and I were partners. Then she told us to spend ten minutes interviewing our partners and, as a trust exercise, to find out one secret about the other person—something that no one in the room knew about them, something that would not be shared with anyone else in class. After that, we were to write short biographies about our partners.

Charles told me about his wife and five children, his home in the rural, far reaches of Greene County, and the church where he was a deacon. I told him about my apartment, my cat, and my trip to Italy with my sister the previous fall—my gift to her for her thirty-fifth birthday.

"What's your secret?" I asked Charles.

"I speak seven languages," he answered without hesitation.

"Wow. Where did you learn seven languages?"

"My parents were missionaries in Haiti and Mexico. That's were I learned French and Spanish. I studied German in college. I was stationed in Saudi Arabia and Okinawa when I was in the marines. So I know Arabic and Japanese."

I watched Charles as he spoke: his legs crossed like chicken wire, bone against bone, his concave chest, his wiry beard hanging from a chin that looked like the edge of a coat hanger. I could not picture this guy as a marine. I had never met any marines, but imagined them to be bigger and more muscular than most people. I'm five-foot-two and I could have taken Charles hostage. But there he sat, smug in his multilingual-ness. I understood a little of the nastiness Anita felt for him.

"That's only six languages," I said.

"Well, I speak *English*. That's seven." He simpered as if whatever secret I could come up with would be banal and un-provocative compared to his.

"What's your secret?" he asked me.

"I'm left-handed," I said, pretty sure that had never come up in any conversation at work.

"That's not a secret. I noticed that the first day I met you," he said. "You've got to come up with something else."

"My real name is not Bitsy."

"I know that. You're on the phone list as *Suzanne*. You're called Bitsy because you're so short. It didn't take a genius to figure that out," he rolled his eyes. "Better come up with something else soon. Time is almost up."

Even if this guy was harmless, he was becoming irritating. "First of all, I'm not *that* short. That's not why I'm called Bitsy. Secondly, I really don't have any secrets, Charles."

"I guess you just have a boring life," he grinned and rubbed his eye under his round glasses.

This guy who had never seen an R-rated movie was calling me boring. One thing I prided myself on was not being a regular, placid, benign thirty-four-year-old woman. I thought of myself as quirky, knowledgeable, and from an interesting—albeit not easy—family. I tried to hear Anita and her partner next to us. Anita was speaking. Her partner, a tiny, quiet Indian woman named Asha, giggled and covered her mouth. I looked across the room and saw one of the technical writers with her jaw hanging open as her partner gestured frantically. Charles and I were the only pair who had stopped talking. He fiddled with his Palm Pilot.

Charles smirked again, "Can't think of anything to shock and amaze me?"

"I'm not in the business of shocking and amazing you," I said,

I looked over toward Anita again. Asha was writing notes while Anita waited. Anita caught my eye, gestured toward Charles—who was not paying attention—and folded her hands in mock prayer. "Time's almost up," Charles said into his Palm Pilot, sounding irritated. It wasn't like he had somewhere else to go. "Come on now," he said. "Even if you bore me to death with it—just tell me a secret."

I folded my arms across my chest.

"My grandmother threw herself out a window in front of my father, with a mincemeat pie baking in the oven." I said.

Charles' lips parted. He bowed his head, put down the Palm Pilot, and covered his face with his hands. His lips moved against his palms. The instructor called time and told us to take a break and then come back and write our partners' bios. Charles uncrossed his legs and turned his chair back toward the conference table without even nodding to me.

Anita and I walked back to our cubes together during the break to check our messages.

"So what was Bible Boy's secret?" she asked me.

"I can't tell you," I answered.

"Oh come on! I'm dying to know what he's keeping from us."

"He speaks seven languages," I answered. I didn't really want to chatter with Anita. I was feeling cold, clammy, and shocked by Charles' silent reaction. How could I have blurted that out? "I have to see if I got e-mail about the new build."

"Nobody did. Everyone was in that class this morning. No one had time to send e-mail."

I ignored her and unlocked my monitor. She waited for me to say something else, and then said in a wounded tone, "I'm going outside for a cigarette."

The rest of the day passed, and I did not have to work alone with Charles again.

That Saturday, my mother called and asked me to go with her to the cemetery the following Sunday to put flowers on my father's grave for the first anniversary of his death. I had put the whole strange incident with Charles out of my mind until then.

"Okay," I said.

"Okay, what?"

"Okay. I'll go with you," I was sad, and not only about my father.

"Well, I'm not asking you to go to the moon. I'm asking you to visit your father's grave on the anniversary of his death. It's not like I ask a lot of you. Ever. I can't ask your brothers to take a five-hour flight here. I can't ask your sister to leave two kids and a husband and drive here from Maryland. Somehow I thought I could ask you. But I guess it's too much."

"It's not too much, Mom. I'll go with you."

"Then what are you pouting about?"

"Not about this," I said.

"Then what the hell is the matter with you?"

"I... I didn't do something that I was supposed to do, that's all"

"What?"

"Nothing."

"What? You're all in a funk about *something*. Why don't you just tell me what it is?"

"Do you remember when you told me Daddy's mother had killed herself?"

"I never told you that. Maybe your father did. Or maybe his goofy aunt did. But I sure didn't. He told me not to tell any of you."

"No, Mom. *You* told me. You and I were the only ones there. *You* told me. And you made me promise not to tell anyone."

"Is there a point to this?"

"I told someone. And I feel kind of bad about it now."

"I hope it wasn't Maureen. You know how damned dramatic she is."

"It was someone at work. And I feel bad because Daddy never even told anyone in our family."

"Bitsy, your father is dead. What difference does it make who told what to who. He's six feet in the dirt. It's not like he can make a fuss about it that the rest of us have to listen to for Chrissake."

"I'll call you in a few days about Sunday," I said and hung up.

Monday morning I was in the break room pouring coffee when I felt a presence hovering over me like I was an obstacle in its path. I set the pot down and turned. Charles blinked at me from behind his round glasses, holding his coffee mug as if I might try to take if from him. We exchanged bland, uncomfortable pleasantries, and then he said, "I just want to let you know that I am praying for you. My wife and I have included you in our prayer circle."

"Well, thank you. And what did I do to deserve that honor?" I asked, laughing politely.

"We're praying for your soul," he answered and pushed past me to pour his coffee. "We're trying to save you from the fires of hell. We're praying that God will show you His mercy and spare you and your loved ones from being punished for the sin of your grandmother."

"What do you mean?" I asked. I didn't even understand enough to be angry.

"Your grandmother is in Hell for the sin of taking her own life. We're asking the Lord to spare you and your loved ones."

Someone else walked into the room and scooted around Charles and me to get to the coffee pots. I stared at Charles as if I had never seen a beard before and waited for the other person to leave the break room.

"My grandmother's not in Hell."

Charles scratched his beard and looked down at me as if I were an imbecile to be pitied rather than scorned. Sitting down together the previous day we had been the same size; standing, he was so much taller than I.

"I'm afraid she is, Bitsy."

"Oh, you've talked to her there?" I said, hot coffee splashing onto my shaking hand. "She sent you a postcard? You know, because *we*, her *family*, never hear from her."

Charles shook his head. "The commandments teach us that no one but God has a right to end life. We are not permitted to end lives, even our own. Do you understand? Your grandmother committed murder when she killed herself."

"So who else is in hell? Is anyone in *your* family there?"

"Bitsy, I know this is hard for you. But your grandmother is in hell. Now we will keep praying so that you and your loved ones don't end up there as well. It's all we can do. We'll do it happily because we love you. Christ loves you."

"I'm going to hell too?"

"The book of Daniel, Chapter Nine tells us 'O Lord, in accordance with all Your righteous acts, let now Your anger and Your wrath turn away from Your city Jerusalem; for because of our sins and the iniquities of our fathers, Jerusalem and Your people have become a reproach to all those around us.' We as a people carry with us the sins of our ancestors, which is why we must repent. You see, Bitsy, you *must* repent." He was talking as if he were reading a script. This, I thought, must be what he does as a deacon at his church. He memorizes text and then stands in front of sleepy, scared, shocked people and recites it— like an actor. Although I hadn't been inside a church since my father's funeral, I had been dragged to Mass every Sunday of my childhood and sent to a Catholic school. I thought I knew a thing or two about scripture.

"That's not what that means!" I yelped.

Anita walked by, looked into the break room, and then kept walking.

"I'm afraid it is," he said calmly. "We are all carrying the sins of our fathers. But Jesus loves us and will forgive us if we repent."

"Well, now I hope I die before Charles Manson. I'd hate it if he got a better room than me in Hell!"

"Bitsy…"

I turned toward the door, and then looked back at him, "How do you say 'You're full of shit' in Japanese?"

After I sat down in my cube, Anita came by with a photocopy of an article about automated testing tools. "I see that you and the Apostle of Christ have formed an unholy alliance," she said.

"He's a jackass," I said to her.

"I told you *that* four years ago," she said.

"Well, I should have listened four years ago."

She waited for me to explain—to tell her how I had discovered that she was right—but I couldn't. It would mean I'd have to tell the secret again. Break my promise again. I didn't have the energy for it.

"Like I told you, he's pure evil," she said.

"I don't think he is, actually," I said. "He seems to really believe he's doing the right thing."

"Nothing's more dangerous than the wrong person thinking they're doing the right thing. You two must have had a special moment together," she said sarcastically.

Charles was in the status meeting that afternoon. But he walked past me the way he would walk past the photocopy machine—not deliberately ignoring me, but having no reason to acknowledge me. I considered accepting his offer of prayers. The next morning, I started to write him an e-mail titled "My grandmother's name was Rose." But I deleted it. I didn't need him to pray for her. Or me either, for that matter.

Kathryn Hawkins was born and raised in Pittsburgh and returned to attend law school after a five-year stint in Santa Cruz, California. Her poetry has appeared in the online journal, Stirring: A Literary Collection.

Girls

BY KATHRYN HAWKINS

We waver, petal-thin, hovering in humming crowds.
Schoolgirl skirts ride up our thighs that shine
like sun through San Francisco fog. Our lips
learn the pout, pucker, and prick. Raspberry red
wine coolers at sleepovers, cigarettes snuck
from someone's cousin's pocketbook. We tear
our ancient posters down. White crescents in our blouses
throw light across the room. We tentatively tongue
boys with gunmetal mouths, fingers inching
toward their zippers and what feels like stones
bulging at the pockets. We sense the current
we create, the heads that swerve to chase
the breeze that dances past our knees.
We scarcely fit in our skins.
Shining locks secure our diaries and doors,
and we don't speak to mothers anymore.

Randall DeVallance is a 2002 graduate of Edinboro University. His short stories have appeared in The Anteater, McSweeney's Online, Eyeshot, Facsimilation, *and many other publications online and in print. A short novel,* Dive, *is forthcoming from Exquisite Cadaver Press. He lives in Pittsburgh.*

Death or Something Like It

BY RANDALL DeVALLANCE

If you think we were just careless kids who got what we deserved, then you've got it all wrong. We knew about protection and had used it right from the beginning. For the first two years it was birth control, but then Marta dropped out of school and wasn't covered by her mother's insurance anymore. We couldn't afford the pill, so I started using condoms. I found a size that wasn't too loose or too tight, and even picked up some pamphlets from the doctor's office to make sure I was putting it on the right way. Four years, we had been together. Then one time, one freak instance, something went wrong. The condom broke, or there was a leak. Who knows? What I do know is that it wasn't our fault. We were monogamous. We used protection. We did everything right. It was mathematics that got us. Pure chance. So how could you blame us for our decision?

The morning of the appointment I got in my car and drove to the suburbs to pick Marta up. We had gotten into a vicious fight the week before, and she had packed her things and moved back home with her mother. The latter wasn't fond of me, and when I pulled up in front of the house I could see her peering through the curtains like some inverted peeping tom. Marta was sitting on the front steps in sweatpants and a baggy T-shirt. She climbed inside and kissed me on the cheek. "I really appreciate this," she said, as we pulled away.

There was no parking lot at the clinic. I found a space two blocks away, near the river. The moment we got out of the car, a stiff breeze smacked us in the face. The weather service was calling for rain, and the neighborhood reflected it, everything sagging, drooping, dragging along—the buildings, the cars, the people, the birds—all smothered beneath an endless gray pall. I locked the doors and reached for Marta's hand. She gave it to me freely, and we wandered along in silence, the shriek of the wind through the alley saying everything that needed to be said.

The clinic was in a black neighborhood, which kept most of the protesters away. Only two, grayhaired men stood out front as we rounded the corner. Each held a cardboard sign pointed towards the street, shouting warnings to the passing cars of the evil taking place in the building behind them. When we came within view, one of the men left his post and scampered over to us, shoving his sign in our faces.

"It's not too late!" he wailed. "Give yourself to Jesus! Your baby inside is begging you!"

His sign was covered with pictures of aborted fetuses; tiny bodies ripped to shreds on cold, steel laboratory tables. Above the pictures were the words "Fetuses are Human Beings" written in magic marker. Julia kept her eyes on the sidewalk as we passed him. I switched sides to shield her from the old man, holding her close around the waist.

"I can see I'm getting through to you," said the old man, following along beside us. "You know in your heart that what you're about to do is wrong! Do you want to live out the rest of your life as a killer?"

Letting go of Marta, I grabbed the sign from his hands and flung it like a Frisbee into the street.

"You bastard!" he screamed, as car after car ground his message of salvation into the pavement. I gave him the finger and went inside.

We stood at the foot of a stairwell, bathed in an eerie half-light. An armed guard waited on the third step, leaning against the handrail as she thumbed through a magazine. She was dressed in full police regalia and resembled a bulldog on its hind legs: short, wide shouldered, and an expressionless face that showed a propensity for both warmth and violence. As we shut the door behind us, she put down her magazine and eyed us with suspicion.

"Name?" she barked.

"Marta McAllister," said Marta.

The guard picked up a clipboard and scrolled through the list of appointments. When she found Marta's name she made a check mark beside it. Instantly, her manner grew softer, and she spoke in an almost motherly tone.

"Is this your husband?" she asked Marta.

"Boyfriend."

"And what's your name, dear?"

"Arthur," I said.

The guard smiled and took our IDs. One after the other, Marta and I climbed up to the third step and emptied our pockets into a large Tupperware bowl lying on the floor.

"Face the wall, arms at ninety degrees," said the guard, waving a metal-detector over every inch of our bodies. We came up clean, and she handed our possessions back.

"Up the stairs," said the guard. "First door on your left. Go right to the desk and sign in."

Marta and I began the long ascent, the guard smiling at us from below like a mother sending her kids off to prom. Three floors up we found the door we wanted and stepped into an air-conditioned office. Directly across from us was a receptionist's desk. The rest of the room opened up on the left into a waiting area, with chairs lining the walls and a coffee table smothered in magazines in the center.

While Marta went to sign in, I picked out a place for us to sit. The chairs in the waiting room were tiny wooden things like you would find in a kindergarten classroom. I sat down and found myself staring at my kneecaps.

Two women were in the waiting room with me. By their age, I guessed they were mothers, whose daughters had already gone back to the operating rooms. One of the women, a frail, stringy-haired blonde, was stroking the sides of her mouth the way a man might stroke his beard, pausing now and again to rifle through her purse. Across the room, a buxom brunette chomped on a piece of gum, studying the ridges of her fingernails.

When Marta saw me she laughed. She was holding a pair of clipboards and handed one to me.

"They told me to have the father fill this out if he was present," she said. "They just want your consent in writing so you can't try to sue them later." She flipped the form over. "Plus, there are some survey questions on the back."

My stomach felt hollow. I took my pen and signed all the forms without reading them. The survey questions were all 'yes' or 'no'. I answered 'yes'. When I was finished I set the clipboard on the seat next to me and held my head in my hands, as the blond woman stroked the sides of her mouth and the brunette chomped her gum.

When Marta finished, we took the forms up to the girl at the desk. She told us to wait some more. I skimmed through the magazines, settling on a battered copy of *Newsweek* from over a decade ago. Marta stared out the window.

When her name was finally called, we both stood and walked across the room. "Not you," said the receptionist, pointing at me. I turned around and went back to my seat. "Don't worry," said the brunette as I passed her by. "She just has to talk to the shrink. It's standard procedure."

An hour later they called for me. I crossed the room again and stood in front of the counter while the girl fumbled through a stack of papers.

"Oh, not there," she said, looking up. "Come around through the swinging doors."

I did as I was told and found myself in a long hallway. On my left was another counter at the same workstation. The same girl rolled her chair over to where I was standing and smiled.

"Here we are, sir!"

"What's the difference between this counter and the one out there?" I asked.

"This one is the pay station."

"I'm not paying! I'm just here for moral support."

"God, I know… " She nodded sympathetically.

"But it seems like your wife… "

"She's not my wife."

"Oh, I'm sorry. Your girlfriend… "

"She isn't my girlfriend, either."

"Well, sir, it seems your *friend* was a little short on her payment."

"How much?"

The girl looked down at the stack of papers again and punched some numbers into a calculator. "Let's see… it looks like… $33."

I paid her the money and was sent to a second waiting room at the end of the hallway. It was similar to the first, with the same chairs and ratty magazines, only much smaller. On the far wall was a door with a sign that read 'WARNING! AUTHORIZED PERSONNEL ONLY' in blood-red lettering.

Further down the hall, another door opened, and Marta emerged with a new stack of forms in her hand. She handed me a clipboard as she came into the room and sat down.

"They want you to fill out this sheet to see if you're psychologically prepared for the after-effects of the operation," she said. "Don't worry, it's all multiple choice."

Marta seemed in good spirits as we filled out the questionnaires. We played what we called the "picture game." One of us would draw a random shape on the back of a piece of paper, and the other person had to change it into a picture. I turned my shape into a helicopter. Marta made hers into a kangaroo.

Two other couples were in the waiting room. Seated across from us was a white woman in her mid-twenties, leaning her head against her boyfriend, a black man, who looked to be a few years older. They were talking about a mutual friend of theirs and laughing at something he had said at a party a few weeks earlier. Suddenly, the woman burst into tears. She pressed her face into the man's chest and wept uncontrollably. I glanced over at Marta to see her reaction, but she only looked at me and made a face. After a few minutes of tears and comforting words from her boyfriend, the woman calmed down and began to laugh again. This happened several more times while we waited, and soon it became part of the background noise, like the nurses' talking or the radio playing "Owner of a Lonely Heart" over the intercom, and we ignored them altogether.

To our right was a Korean couple. They kept their faces pointed forward, refusing to look at one another. The girl's face was a swollen mess. Tears seeped from the corners of her eyes, running out around her cheekbones and collecting at the jaw where they dripped down to stain her white, cotton blouse. Her body trembled from time to time as she strained to cover up her sobbing. At one point I noticed her sneak a glance in her boyfriend's direction. His eyes never wavered. They were locked on some random point on the far wall, his face tense with anger and shame. Marta and I forgot about them. Certain things had to be done, so why not smile and laugh and rail against the absurdity of it all?

Once more, Marta's name was called, and once more, I was told to remain seated. She took the clipboards with her and disappeared behind another closed door. I was just settling in for a long wait when a woman in a lab coat appeared and ushered me into the same room Marta had gone into. A sign on the door read "217: Staff Psychologist's Office."

The Staff Psychologist's Office turned out to be a converted broom closet, with some potted plants and a file cabinet in place of the cleaning equipment. Against the far wall was a desk. Behind the desk sat a neatly dressed woman in her forties, her hair trimmed short and business-like. For the life of me, I couldn't figure out how she had gotten back there. The desk was so wide it touched the walls on either side of the room. She would have had to either crawl underneath on her hands and knees or climb overtop of it. Either way, it wasn't the sort of thing that inspired confidence in a physician.

A pair of metal folding chairs were arranged facing the desk. On the back were the words "Property of St Michael's Church" stenciled in black ink. I looked at Marta, who smiled at me as I sat down.

The nameplate on the woman's desk read "Barb Wittenour." She waited until I was situated before speaking.

"Hello Arthur," she said, with a rehearsed warmth

she must have learned from one of her manuals. "I've been talking to Marta here to see if she has any concerns about the procedure, and now I'd like to talk to you as well."

She flipped through the papers on her desk until she found my questionnaire. "From your answers, you seem to handling things very well."

"Thank you," I said.

"Do you have any questions or concerns you'd like to talk with me about?"

"Not really."

Barb nodded. "Good enough for me. When you go out the door, turn immediately to your left. You'll see a small room with a TV set and some chairs. You can wait there until the doctor's ready for you."

We thanked Barb and got up to leave. Out in the hall, we turned to our left and found the waiting room exactly where she said it would be. We went in and picked out a place to sit.

In one of the corners was a TV set, showing a video on a continuous loop. We were too busy gawking at the walls to pay any attention. Every square-inch of free space had been covered with pink, paper cutouts of fetuses baring messages of hope and comfort from former patients. A rather large fetus assured

us that God was on our side, so there was no reason
to worry. Another, more modest fetus told us how
happy it was to have been aborted, because now it
was in Heaven with the angels instead of languishing
in an orphanage. One of the more creative patients
had used a marker to give their fetus a face (complete
with elfin grin) and had altered its tiny hands into a
thumbs-up. On its chest were the words "Keep
Smiling." I didn't know whether to laugh or cry.

Marta stirred in the seat next to me. She asked me
if I would play with her hair. It was the only thing
that calmed her down when she was feeling nervous.
I asked her how she was doing.

"I'm just afraid it's going to hurt," she said.
A woman in sky-blue nurse's scrubs appeared to take
Marta to the operating room. Marta asked her if I
could go in with her.

"Once you're situated, he's more than welcome to
sit with you," she said.

"Oh, will you Arthur? Please?"

"Sure," I said.

Marta smiled and followed the nurse down the
hall to another closed door. The nurse waited outside while Marta went in to get undressed. Soon she
was joined by another nurse and then another, and

another, and finally, by a tall, imposing man in a white lab coat and surgical mask. From his air of authority I took him to be the doctor. He pointed at some charts he was holding. Then he pointed to one of the rooms. He pointed at the patients, pointed at the walls, at the ceiling, the floor, the windows, the fake plants. He pointed at everything he could find. The nurses followed his every move like trained seals. He was a lucky guy, old Doc. They were a very pretty bunch of nurses.

Behind me was a picture window looking down on the street. I watched the people wandering the sidewalk, some stopping at the convenience store on the corner for cigarettes or something cold to drink before continuing on, out of my range of view and lost forever. Some had interesting faces; some didn't. I didn't give it much thought. I knew there would always be others wandering in to take their places.

A different nurse came for me, a German nurse who spoke tersely and had wide, powerful hips that swished from side to side when she walked. I followed those hips down the hall to the operating room. The door was opened; I was ushered inside. A chorus of stares greeted me as I stepped over the threshold. Marta, the doctor, the nurses... all of them fixed their eyes on me and waited, as if expecting me to juggle or say something witty. I could feel the eyes of the German nurse too, pounding my skull from behind. I moved out of the way so she could come in and shut the door.

"How are *you*?" asked the doctor, walking away before I could answer. He still had his surgical mask on, so that all you could see was his eyes as he skimmed over Marta's charts.

Marta was stretched out on a leather table, the top end elevated slightly like a recliner. At the other end, situated between her legs, were a stool, a halogen lamp, and a surgical tray holding an assortment of jagged, metal equipment. I sat there dumbly holding Marta's hand, wishing I could think of something profoundly comforting to say.

"All right," said the doctor, sitting down. "How are we doing today, Marta?"

"Not bad, considering... "

"Considering," the doctor nodded. "That's right." He scanned the surgical tray and picked out a flat, rectangular device that looked like a paint scraper. "If you've been to the gynecologist you're probably familiar with this," he said, holding it up.

The doctor leaned forward, hidden by the sheet

that covered Marta from the waist down. She drew in a deep breath and her eyes grew wide.

"Are you okay?" I asked, squeezing her hand.

"I'm fine. The metal was cold, that's all."

The doctor brought the halogen lamp down and shone it between Marta's legs. Then he switched it off and leaned back in his seat. "Fine," he said. "Just fine." Putting the paint scraper aside, he reached down to the floor and came back with a long metal rod that looked like an umbrella handle. On one end was a rubber hose, connected to a small generator beneath the doctor's chair. The doctor held the rod up towards the ceiling and pressed a lever near its base, producing a brittle hissing like the sound of a service station air pump.

"This next part is simple," he said. "I'm going to go inside you with this device here… " He held up the metal rod. "And basically suck out all the pieces of fetal tissue. It's a very quick procedure. During it you'll feel a sharp pain that resembles a bad case of menstrual cramps. Let me know if it becomes too severe."

Doc disappeared behind the sheet again. Marta's hand hovered over mine, ready to clamp down if the pain became too much.

"All right," said the doctor. "Now that everything's in place, we'll begin suction… "

The doctor pressed the switch and the machine kicked on. This time, instead of a hissing, there was a mushy, slurping noise. It reminded me of a milkshake getting sucked through a straw. Marta's eyes rolled back in her head. Her hand gripped mine so hard I was sure something had been broken. Sweat was breaking out across her forehead. The muscles in her arms began to tremble. I was about to yell for the doctor to stop, when Marta clenched her jaw and settled herself, drawing in deep breaths through her nose. I leaned over her, wanting to offer some encouragement, but everything that came to my head sounded vague and insincere.

Despite my better judgment, I waited until none of the nurses were looking and peeked my head around the edge of the sheet. The doctor was holding the vacuum inside of Marta, peering between her legs, just as I had expected. Only, you could see it. As he moved the rod around, you could see it jabbing up into her skin, raising it from her body like a tent pole. *He's going to kill her*, I thought. I pulled my head back and kept my eyes pointed forward.

The doctor made small talk as he worked. He asked Marta what high school she had gone to, where she worked, and all the other boring questions you get asked by strangers in uncomfortable situations. Marta answered them all, her voice trembling from the exertion. When the doctor mentioned it might rain, I was sure he was some kind of sadist, and I could feel my skin grow hot as I prepared to tell him off. But it worked. Soon they were jabbering back and forth as if nothing was the matter. Marta's breathing grew more even, her muscles relaxed, and she even took her hand away from mine to brush back her hair.

And then, it was all over. The doctor turned off the machine and told Marta she was the toughest patient he'd ever operated on. Then he disappeared, mask and all, bounding out the door in a cloud of mystery. The rest of us filed out after him so Marta could get dressed.

Outside, the skies had finally opened up. I stood at the window in the lobby, watching the thin but steady drizzle send everyone running for cover. Rain began collecting at the edge of the street, forming a miniature stream that ran along the curb and disappeared through the sewer grate on the corner.

Marta appeared through the swinging doors, a nurse holding her arm and leading her along in swollen baby-steps. I hurried across the room to take over.

"Is there any more paperwork or can we go?" I asked.

"You're all set," said the nurse. She smiled. "I think it's sweet you came to support your girlfriend. I wish more men would take responsibility for their actions."

I toed the ground, feeling like some sort of fraud, but Marta smiled too and reached for my hand. I took her by the arm and led her out the door, then down each of the steps, one by one, to the street below. Outside, the sidewalk was deserted.

"Are you in a lot of pain?" I asked.

"It's just like when I get cramps," she said. "My legs are really stiff though."

We hadn't remembered to bring an umbrella, but neither of us minded. The rain felt cool against our skin. As we turned the corner we passed a group of children playing in the street, their clothes soaked through from jumping in the puddles that had collected by the curb. I looked at their young, vibrant bodies and then at the buildings decaying behind them. Neither Marta nor I spoke. It seemed like the right thing to do. I'd like to say we were being reflective, but the truth is, I could only think about what I was going to do next, whether to go out or stay in for the night, whether to grab a bite to eat or make something at home. I don't know what Marta was thinking. Maybe she did the mourning for both of us.

Another block up we saw a pair of men standing around an old station wagon. It was the protesters. They were loading their signs into the trunk, their day finished now that the four o'clock appointments had all made it safely inside. From the looks on their faces it hadn't been a successful afternoon.

As we passed them, I braced myself for one final confrontation, but all the zeal, all the hope from earlier in the afternoon was gone, replaced by wet, sagging shoulders and slow, shuffling steps. One of the men, eyes fixed on the sidewalk, snuck a look in our direction. He shook his head but didn't say anything, no insults or condemnations. We simply weren't worth it.

Nothing could be done now anyway. The signs were packed up in the car. Another potential life had been lost. In the end, something had to die. We decided to save ourselves.

Karl Elder is Lakeland College's Poet in Residence and author of four volumes of poetry from Prickly Pear Press, including Phobophobia *and* A Man in Pieces. *Two new books will appear from Parallel Press and Marsh River Editions in 2005. Among his honors are a Pushcart Prize, the Lucien Stryk Award, grants from the Illinois Arts Council for poetry and fiction, and Lakeland's Outstanding Teacher Award.*

The Strip

BY KARL ELDER

Karl invents a comic strip in which
he becomes his own character. At first
it will not be a secret, and he sketches
it with little gusto—something to do on
a rainy Saturday for which his mate takes
no notice. Weeks pass and amazingly Karl
has a pile of drawings among work papers
he knows not how to explain. Now he
is startled when his wife walks into
the room, and he is observed quickly
shuffling his desktop should people
call to say they are stopping over.
One day some people in the comic strip
call to say they are stopping over.
Karl goes into a panic. There are
drawings flying everywhere, one of which
slips out the open window and lands
like a big leaf at Karl's wife's feet
where she is raking. "What is *this*?"
she wants to know, thrusting the drawing

in the face of Karl, who's spun in
his chair next to the window where
she stands in the threshold of the door.

Terrified, Karl erases the evidence
and, since her hand holds the drawing,
also part of her arm. Soon she is standing
there, not all there, a trace of her former
self imbued with a beauty he formerly could
only imagine. Over her head Karl fashions
a light bulb dark as an eclipse of the moon.
Within a year there is a bale of paper
so thinly dispersed about their house
it cannot possibly be detected, for Karl
has long ago arrived at an answer why he
started the strip in the first place—
his desk never exactly the same in
consecutive frames, a seemingly endless
variety of kitchen aids, portraits
on the walls all originals in halls
and corridors that must wind through
space for the length it would take
decades to tour, the walls themselves
only the obverse of more walls behind
which is every model of every object he

ever desired, not the least of which is
Karl, a transformed man, drawn now
with a knowledge bump on top of his head,
the head which still houses its secret.

Jessica Mesman is a freelance writer and the managing editor of the literary journal Creative Nonfiction. *Her work has appeared in* Godspy, Brevity, *and* The New Yinzer *and is forthcoming from* Riverteeth *and* Elle.

Family Secret

BY JESSICA MESMAN

His room had no television, and the double bed was made up with a polyester bedspread that held on to my hair when I slept. It was the worst place to sleep in my grandmother's house. The walls were blank except for a crucifix, which hung over the bed's headboard and reminded me of the one in *A Nightmare on Elm Street*, the one that keeps jumping off the wall right before Tina dies. Our uncle slept in this room when he got weekend passes from the VA Hospital. Otherwise he spent most of his time sitting at the kitchen table, staring and smoking.

About once a month, my sister and I took turns riding with my grandmother to Biloxi to pick up our uncle, a real chore because Biloxi was two hours away and our grandmother chain-smoked Kent 100s with the windows rolled up and listened to 1450 AM the whole way, old-people music, Glen Miller and Nat King Cole, tapping her perfect fingernails on the steering wheel and singing along at random, sometimes the lyrics, sometimes her own hypnotizing "Choom,

choom... Choom, choom... " as she shrugged her shoulders with the beat.

I was in it for Sonic burgers with mustard and a stop at the bookstore for a couple of new editions of *Sweet Valley High*. We worked on this kind of reward system: stop biting your nails and I'll buy you a ring with your birthstone; ten dollars for every "A" on your report card. I had few friends and no plans to interfere, so I often took my sister's shifts too. My grandmother liked this about me, and I milked it. I liked playing the martyr. This was around the time that I started wearing my sweater and jacket all day long at school to see if I could stand the heat.

The drive was boring, but the hospital was painful. It smelled like pee. Murals of weapon-toting soldiers in fatigues covered the walls. The residents looked dirty and vaguely criminal; they scared and embarrassed me when we walked past the rooms where they watched TV and they nodded in recognition, or worse, shouted out "Hey, Ms. Frances!" to which my grandmother smiled and responded, "Well, hey!" and waved back with big, gracious flaps of her wrist, as if to fans beyond a velvet rope.

She liked to make a lot of noise on the way to my uncle's room—typical showboating on her part, I thought. This was the woman who called the gas station to let them know that Frances Arnold was coming in to fill up the tank. The woman who had two mink coats in a city where, for 25 years, it had not snowed a single flake. She liked big entrances.

Or maybe she thought it was best to warn my uncle of her arrival. Maybe she was afraid of what she might catch him doing in there.

I don't know why she worried because every time, we found him sitting on the edge of his bed and waiting for us with his overnight bag at his feet, as if he'd been sitting there and waiting for us since we'd dropped him off a month before. He would be dressed in one of those all-in-one jumpsuits from Sears. I've never seen anyone else wear one in real life—only characters in movies who are supposed to be appear hopelessly out of step with time, like Samantha's grandpa Ed in *Sixteen Candles*. His hair would be neatly combed, his shoes shined. He'd smell of Old Spice.

Recognition took a moment. For a long time, my sister and I thought he was retarded, but now I know it was the Thorazine that made him slow. Despite all my grandmother's hooting and peacocking and the overnight bag packed at his feet, he always looked surprised to see us.

She'd knock twice on his open door and call out, "Hey my baby!" She called him baby and Deedle and Bubba, which is what we called him, but never his real name, Cyril, which she hated. Cyril was my grandfather's name. Bubba was the oldest child, older than my mom by seventeen years, and my grandmother's favorite because he needed her the most.

My grandparents had a rocky marriage, lived out in separate bedrooms on opposite sides of the house. He referred to her in conversation as "the ol' bitch." My sister says she once saw my grandmother aim for his head with the old rotary phone that sat on their kitchen counter. What I remember is this: an old picture I found in her bedroom of him pinching her boob. They were both laughing, something I don't think I ever saw them do together in real life. And I remember this: When he died, my grandmother stood in front of the mausoleum wall, shaking her fist at his grave like a soap opera villain and yelling "I can't believe you beat me to it!"

Bubba would laugh a weak, slow laugh as she kissed his cheek and announced too loudly, as if talking to a foreign-exchange student or a child, "Look who came to see you!"

JESSICA MESMAN

My cue: a weak smile, a tense body offered up for a hug.

"Well, look who it is," he'd say, thick-tongued, and pat me lightly, robotically, on the back. He called my sister and me "the girls," not Jennifer and Jessica, which is a mouthful even if you aren't drugged.

"That's swell."

On the way home, we drove down the Gulf Coast while Bubba smoked his Pall Malls and my grandmother her Kent's. I moved to the backseat and cracked the window every now and then, but if my grandmother noticed she'd yell, "Don't let that Gulf air blow on you," and roll it right back up. Bubba's ashes dusted the Cadillac's white upholstery. He was a sloppy and forgetful smoker. All my grandmother's cars were dotted with constellations of scorches and deep, black pits.

He called her "Mama." His was a different accent than my parents and mine; our words were less elegant, more guttural. *New Awlins. Pecawn. Dawlin.* He was raised in Georgia, and I imagine that he started out with that pretty, sprawling southern accent of my grandmother and her sister and brother. But the drugs distorted Bubba's baritone drawl and made him sound like a caricature, a dumb cracker. "Mawwwwma."

All these things together: the slow, thick, speech and retarded delivery. The dopey nicknames. The hospital. They overshadowed the stacks and shelves of books, the philosophy and literary theory, the theology, the science fiction, the Faerie Queene and the collected Dickens, that filled the shelves in his old bedroom. The saxophone and clarinet in the closet and the piano in the den that he'd once played. Despite it all, we actually thought he was dim.

My grandmother encouraged this: better to be stupid than schizophrenic; better to be physically ill, with "ulcers" and "bad kidneys" than a head case. Nobody talked about the letters he sent home decoding the patterns in our names and birthdays, patterns that revealed our family's connection to the civil war. He started with his own name, Cyril Solomon Arnold– CSA: the Confederate States of America. We couldn't listen to the radio or watch TV because it made Bubba "nervous." TV characters would tell him to crush his eyeglasses under the soles of his Hushpuppies. I never told my grandmother, but when I slept over, I sometimes woke to him sitting on the edge of my bed, watching snow on the television, the sound turned down low. This is the sort of behavior that would land him back in the hospital with no weekend passes.

When he was more stable, he lived in a string of halfway houses for retired vets in Mississippi. The people who ran these places now strike me as the kinds of phonies who are only in it for the money, like abusive and neglectful foster parents. They were full of whispers to my grandmother about Bubba's strange behavior, to which she responded with embarrassed concern.

When we visited, the caretakers usually pulled my grandmother aside for a debriefing. Left alone, Bubba would ask me, "How's school?" Here we go again, I'd think. Always with the school, this guy. And what does a kid ever have to say about school?

"It's fine," I'd reply, and look back down at my shoes and my watch and think about my Sonic burger. "It's *swell.*"

Meanwhile, I was trying to eavesdrop on the hushed conferences.

Bubba's interest in my education seemed superficial at the time, like lame small talk. If I'd known that he was paying the steep tuition for the Catholic school I attended, I might have been more forthcoming with details. But none of us talked about Bubba as a real person, much less as a cultured intellectual or a kind benefactor. Still, all the evidence was there, and I chose to ignore it.

I wasn't allowed to take books out of Bubba's room. My grandmother didn't like it when I dug around in there. This was unspoken but clear. Bubba wasn't allowed to take books out of the room, either. Like the radio and the television, they were off limits, a measure of protection against their potential for transmission of secret messages. They stayed on the shelves, maybe for decoration, or maybe for the day when he returned home for good, cured.

Sometimes he asked for a specific book, requested that my grandmother bring it on the next visit. Usually she wouldn't, but every so often, she couldn't resist. She'd smuggle the book into the hospital in a brown paper bag with his carton of cigarettes, and a week later, one of the nurses would find it and ship it back.

Yet when he was home, with access to an entire library in his own bedroom, I never saw him read. Probably because when he left the hospital for the weekend, his doctors upped his meds to induce a near catatonic trance; otherwise he might start mumbling to himself—*You despise me, don't you?*—at the kitchen table, or sneaking into other people's bedrooms to watch television with the sound down low.

Our family encouraged my sister and me to read, but they bought our books new from the bookstore

or from the newsprint catalogues sent home with us
from school. They arrived with pristine spines, un-
tainted by the conspicuous absence in my uncle's
back bedroom, and their subject matter was appro-
priate for little girls. They were about babysitting
and solving neighborhood mysteries.

Nobody else in my family read or owned books,
though my grandmother read The Enquirer and Star
weekly, bought them every Tuesday when they hit
the checkout line at the supermarket down the street
from her house. One time I went with her on this
weekly errand, and while we waited in line she asked
the woman in front of us if she'd clean her house for
$25 a week. I was mortified, but the woman said yes,
and she cleaned my grandmother's house for the
next ten years. That was Frances's offensive, obnox-
ious power. She thought she could get anyone to do
anything as long as she paid her.

So we were complicit. Knowing, or more to the
point, acknowledging, that Bubba was smart would
have changed everything. So we stayed quiet, and
asked no questions. Besides, if we confirmed our sus-
picions we might have to respect him, get to know
him, make an effort. These were far more demanding
chores than monthly visits and bland conversations

in depressing, embarrassing spaces. And what would it mean to have a crazy uncle instead of a physically sick or even a retarded uncle—a hopeless case? Who would take responsibility? None of us was willing to let go of the easy myth, the deal we'd struck. We kept him stupid and sick, but not contagious.

Which was more than a myth; it was a lie. The chances that my sister and I would be schizophrenic were actually one in four. Those increased with the experience of trauma before the age of twenty-one—like losing a parent. Jennifer told me this over the phone one day when we were both in college. She was working on a master's degree in psychology. I was majoring in English and convinced I was going crazy. Was the recurring refrain of Billy Joel's "Uptown Girl," lodged in my head for months, a symptom of impending dementia? We spent hours on the phone, wondering: What had happened to him? And more important, how had it affected us?

When we talked, we pieced together fragments of information, evidence pooled from overheard conversations, discovered photographs and documents.

We knew that Bubba had been married, briefly, to a woman named Freidel. Whenever my grandmother said her name she spit it out quick, like spoiled food. But my mom had shown me pictures of her once—their wedding shots. She was beautiful with dark hair and big dark eyes. We knew nothing else of their brief marriage or divorce. My mother was still a baby when Friedel disappeared. We have several theories.

THEORY ONE:

Our mother wasn't our grandmother's child at all, but the child of Friedel and Bubba, left for my grandmother to raise after Friedel's sudden departure, which was responsible for Bubba's nervous breakdown.

SUPPORTING EVIDENCE:

Bubba, at our mother's funeral, approaching the casket, my dad and my grandmother supporting him on either side, collapsed when he saw her body. My sister says he sat crying for a long time after, insisting that it should have been him.

"And it should have been," she says, still, when we talk about it long distance on our cell phones in Oklahoma City and Pittsburgh. Our mom was 36 and necessary, and he was a mental vegetable, living most of his days alone and confused in a terrible place.

But what makes this funeral scene seem so important to the whole mystery is its contrast with the events that followed my grandmother's death. My grandmother—Bubba's lifeline, his Pall Mall hookup, his only friend, visitor, and confidante. When she died, my sister and my dad drove to Biloxi to deliver the news. My sister says that when she told him, Bubba looked at her blankly, and when he finally responded, all he said was, "So soon?"

REBUTTAL:

When cleaning out my grandmother's house after her death, I found my mom's birth certificate, which clearly identifies Frances and Cyril A. Arnold, not the Confederate States, as the parents.

"Those things can be faked, you know," my sister argued.

THEORY TWO:

My grandmother drove Bubba insane, and this was why my grandfather hated her.

SUPPORTING EVIDENCE:

My grandfather often brought out the big guns when they were arguing; one of his old standbys, and a personal favorite of my dad's, was "You're the one who turned Bubba into a Christmas turkey." In the time we knew her, our grandmother had proven herself perfectly capable of inciting violence and lapses of reason. She also fancied herself an amateur pharmacist, passing out prescription drugs that she got on the fly from her doctor friends and her pharmacy connection, Dr. Phil, who wasn't a doctor at all. Our dad later implicated her as the source of our mom's supposed Valium addiction. The day that our mom told us she had cancer, my grandmother slipped me a Xanax. I was thirteen.

REBUTTAL:

If my grandmother had the power to permanently destroy someone's mental vigor, we would all be in a hospital.

THEORY THREE:

Bubba's time in the armed forces resulted in post-traumatic stress disorder.

SUPPORTING EVIDENCE:

He was in the Veteran's Hospital.

REBUTTAL:

To our knowledge, the extent of his service in the US Army had been playing saxophone at the USO dances. By Vietnam, he'd been in the hospital for five years. And besides, this was obviously the least intriguing and soap-operatic of all the options. We preferred to imagine our family's story as a hybrid of Greek tragedy and Days of Our Lives. Which brings us to

THEORY FOUR:

The family secret.

SUPPORTING EVIDENCE:

On her deathbed, my grandmother struggled and murmured like a daytime television heroine. One of her more coherent ramblings went something like this:

"Thank God she never found out!"

She might as well have said: "The money's in the…" and then drifted off to the other side. Who was she? Our mom? Friedel? My sister? Me? And what didn't she find out? That she wasn't who she thought she was? That her whole life she's been swinging from the branch of the wrong family tree? My sister and I are convinced that the answers to these questions are the answers to all the questions we have about our family. They will tell us why Bubba lost his mind. And why our mother died young. And why my sister got divorced, and why I can't quit smoking.

I guess we could have asked Bubba. But the last time either of us saw him alive was the day we buried my grandmother in the mausoleum wall between her husband and our mother. Bubba's was the only space left to fill.

That afternoon, my sister and I sat on the patio of my grandmother's house and contemplated Bubba's future. We rarely sat on the patio, though it was lovely as southern patios can be, with red brick and wrought iron and potted plants and a slow, ticking ceiling fan. I'm not sure what Jennifer's reasons were; I'd been scared away by my grandmother's story of some distant relative electrocuted by a lightening bolt on the back porch swing. But Bubba was dominating the living room, snoozing in the swivel-rock recliner, and, with our grandmother gone, there was a sense of unrestricted access to the house. The old cautionary tales lost their teller and their heft.

The house was now ours. But what to do with Bubba? We were so worried that he would crack; we'd been trained for so long to expect the worst from him, to suspect that any moment with him might devolve into an embarrassing disaster, that neither of us had spoken more than a few words to him since he'd arrived.

In a rare moment of sensitivity, my sister's first husband, Scott, urged us to consult our uncle, insisting that Bubba was actually pretty smart; it was our grandmother who made us think we couldn't talk to him. But neither my sister nor I wanted to test this theory. Better to think Bubba was happier in the hospital. Better to think they took good care of him over there. Better to think our visits would be painful reminders of loss. We had lived all our lives with the secret shame of Bubba's illness. And now that he was here without the buffer of our grandmother between him and us, the pressure of being his last remaining heirs rested heavy on both our consciences. I don't think either one of us could wait to deposit him back at the hospital, to take one last smoky trip to Biloxi, and then put it all behind us.

And so that's what we did. Four months later, he was dead.

When we sold our grandmother's house later that year, I took Bubba's books and a couple of his book-cases. I keep them separate from my own books. I think of them as strands of code that, linked with the proper operators, could tell me who he really was, before the Christmas turkey, before the illness, before the character that my grandmother invented to protect herself. When I look at their spines, I wonder which one finally did it—was it the Asimov that pushed him over the edge? The complete set of *Remembrance of Things Past*?

But the more I know, the less gracious I find all of us. The answers to our questions make my family even more fallen and despicable.

JESSICA MESMAN

Knowing that I fully, spectacularly, sinfully failed Bubba, my conscience, or my ego, whispers to me that I can still do right by him. Write, it says. Give him the story he deserves. And yet, it isn't the story I've told here at all—the VA, the stupid nicknames, the drugs, the disregard. To see it all here, I feel even more ashamed. I've wronged him again. I should have written about Cyril, the husband, the musician, the reader. Who knows which one is the fiction?

Besides, no matter how hard I try to describe my family with holy resonance, to write it all down dark and shady, it ends up funny, or funny to me. That's how we worked, I guess. We traded in jokes and sarcasm and sitcoms. I wish that we'd been poetic and reverent, that we'd shared a moment of the sublime. But I can't think of a single time that struck us all speechless. Someone always had something smart-ass to say, some crack to make. We didn't like silence. We slept with televisions on and ceiling fans spinning, habits my sister and I never outgrew. We find it impossible to drift off without the strains of a laugh track or the whir of a fan. We talk too much and laugh too loud.

There is nothing funny about being sick or crazy. Maybe that's why I couldn't talk to my mom after I knew she had cancer, and why I never talked to Bubba about books, and why I never demanded our true story from anybody. Now I am sick with regret for all of it. I try to trace the line from Proust to pressed jumpsuits to faked birth certificates to "Thank God she never found out" to how I'm tall, like Bubba, even though my mom and dad were both short, but I only end up with a list of all the things I don't know or I'm too afraid to admit. And my sister's tired of talking about it anyway.

All I can write is this: I'm sorry, Bubba. In the end, I'm like your mother; I decided on this version because I couldn't bear the others.

Don Kingfisher Campbell is the founder of POETRYpeople youth writing workshops, publisher of the San Gabriel Valley Poetry Quarterly, *and leader of the Emerging Urban Poets writing and critique workshop. He received the 2001 Charles Ferguson Prize from the Pennsylvania Poetry Society, among other awards, and his poetry appears in several anthologies, including* Cosmic Brownies *and* Three Chord Poems.

Vomiting for God

BY DON KINGFISHER CAMPBELL

first go

to get out
of your head
with your "friends"

your drinking
buddies

eat more pizza slices
than one hand
can count

don't forget
the anchovies

guzzle some
beer, try

different brands

with each heavy glassy
overpriced mug

especially the Moosehead

perform repeatedly
the Heineken maneuver

don't stop until
you feel like stealing
someone else's jacket

make a sign of the cross

forgive yourself

then drive

homeward bound, yelling
to a song, it's

"More Than a Feeling"
blasting out of your car
radio, windows down
rushing night

DON KINGFISHER CAMPBELL

air closing sweating
pores, think you're lucky

no cop saw you
find historical ways

to piss
off glinting chrome

make drumbeats
with Botts dots

creep
into your apartment

quietly lie

in the already dark bed-
room

form a mummy's X

go to "sleep"

wait

for that positively
earthly

rumbling in your stomach

turn your head
back and forth like
an anchovy

when backwash comes
knocking at your esophagus

run excitedly to the john

open your mouth

and watch all evil
thoughts spill out
past your teeth:

the times you wore
plaid bell-bottoms

and exchanged
childish fists

DON KINGFISHER CAMPBELL

to exact revenge
for being born

a middle class
little sphincter,

that summer sunburned
teenager sneaking

into *Saturday Night
Fever* matinees,

equally inane quasi-adult
five-fingering pizza

from an unoccupied table
near the restroom,

getting married
because you had Catholic sex

with the first girl out
of boys' high school,

leering at the married

mother of two

who smiles when you pass
her at the entrance

to your complex,

wonder why
you didn't fuck

that poet
who wanted you,

the year
you considered voting
Republican;

these seven guttural sins,
each open-mouthed, cry

as infidelities past
pass into the unfeeling

uncaring cold porcelain
receptive bowl

DON KINGFISHER CAMPBELL

chunky flecks
of disbelief in God
fall

(hear yourself
pray "Oh God
I'll never do this again")

kneel
and observe

globs
of lies

told in your life
that now seem like

bell peppers,

sway deliriously
like an insignificant fly,

egg on
the heaving urge

for continuing
animal roar

of flowing tongue,
chant out loud

when you pass
midnight

recreate all past
California stops

those wonderful
stolen moments

you'll never forget, each time
you twitch

for the Lord's forgiveness

praise the invention
of man

unloading
eating sin

DON KINGFISHER CAMPBELL

in a sacred
hole

Holly Farris is an Appalachian who has worked as an autopsy assistant, restaurant baker, and beekeeper. To date, she has published close to sixty articles, poems, and stories, including erotica. Her newest short fiction is forthcoming from Frontiers: A Journal of Women's Studies *and* Home Planet News.

Midway

BY HOLLY FARRIS

I counted the trip underway as soon as Sister
Josephine's liver-spotted hand fluttered out the car
window to wave, just as she turned up my gravel
road. Eighteen years old, country girl and a convict,
I was headed out on official business with her, a
Catholic sister four times my age, at the wheel.

Everyone laid off from the furniture factory, men
and women at home watching Regis and Kathy Lee,
peeked out around flowery curtains in their living
rooms and kitchens. Nosy neighbors could have mem-
orized the government license numbers on her
Virginia Department of Social Services Escort, their
eyes bugged out so much.

Sister Josephine, my boss that summer at Social
Services, had thrown me a bone. "This trip to Virginia
Beach is your pay for June and July," she had said. A
work trip was hardly running away from Bland
County's mountains, something I considered regu-
larly. Early on the morning we left, all I let myself be

was bored. We'd ride forever while she drove the state car, pretend to work during the day, and sleep in a hotel room that she and I would share for exactly one night.

What little I did in her office was licking envelopes and minding children, talents that earned me zero paycheck. I dandled dirty-diapered babies, black and white the same, on my knee while their mommas begged for food stamps. Babies drooled silver spit threads wherever they had a notion on the ripped leatherette sofa outside the main office. When I first met her, Jo had talked stern to me about community service, the hours I had to serve. "Or else," she said. Social Services was summer prison; Jo was the matron.

At least some of my crime had run in the newspaper for everyone to see. Before I graduated high school (the last thing I did that Bland approved of), my best friend Marva Woods and I went to Wal-Mart of a Friday night. I remember it as her idea, shocking because she's the judge's daughter, but somehow a mascara tube plus two colors of eye shadow in one tray, colored pools beside a tiny magic wand, wound up in my pocket. Wouldn't you know, like in a small town, it was Marva's father who sentenced me to community service. People said it was even chances I'd grow into the same type of criminal my momma was.

Idling in my gravel road's turn-around space before we took off, Jo set my boxy make-up case and paper Kroger sack with clothes alongside her plastic suitcase in the car's trunk. From the very minute she slammed down the lid, she counted on us following her Social Services plan, but I prayed for alternative inspiration. Taking her out of the office might let me work more sympathy than I usually got out of her. Or I could run.

"I'm ready, Jo," I said. I yawned, clapping a hand over my lip-glossed mouth. I straddled the dirt scab beside our house where my brother, who's my guardian because momma died in prison, parks. He rests eighteen truck wheels there on weekends if he's earned enough miles during the week hauling.

When he had seen me packing my case, my brother kept his eyes on the TV. Middle August—when anyone, consecrated or not, craved cold air blasting out a car's dash—was not an ideal time to travel. My new Plum Crazy lipstick rode in the top cosmetics tray, cuddled between dividers. That removable plastic layer reminded me of expensive foam plates some people carry to picnics. "Rita," my brother called out over the personal injury ad blaring on TV, "I've been everwhere has freight and the onliest place sets comfortable is this sofa."

If I had a bad family and community situation, I knew Jo had it worse. Poor soul, she had lived inside a convent until she got so old they let her out, until boys or make-up were no thrill for her. From what Jo said, the convent sounded like women's prison, singing and prayers all the weekdays. The only thing I envied of hers was the nickname, short and direct.

Leaving on a trip had to be familiar to a boss lady, but she fretted as soon as I sat in the passenger seat. "Joseph watches over me on trips," she said right off. "He sees to restaurants, parking, check-in." Since we were the only two in her department, the head guy being Mike, I couldn't guess who she meant. "Joseph is the human father of Jesus, my patron saint," she explained soft, nice, like church work makes nuns talk.

Some of the crap Jo says can be used cussing. I thought I'd test-cuss *Father of Jesus* that very evening. I needed to get the words ready, make it sound natural for use around my friends back home in Bland County. My boyfriend Dwain, who appreciates good cussing, has never been out of Bland. Right before the trip, he gave me a ring to wear, partly to make sure I came home. Actually, he might have been jealous, at least more than my brother was, because Dwain had said to me, "Rita, you got no job. You got a sentence."

Signs I watched for as Jo drove out of Bland were *Congratulations Gradutes!* at the Blood Bought Christian Daycare. I wondered if Jo would laugh at the sign and was just as happy she didn't. I wasn't as holy as her, but I had learned to spell. We saw *GO Bless America* at the high school (they lost their *D* my junior year), and *Feel Dirt,* jagged in spray paint, at the ramp leading onto the interstate. The last was my favorite, not that I see the sense in carrying dirt from one hole to another.

Once we hit Virginia Beach's main street, I read the turns written between creases on her Social Services paper. "Left, right, right again," was the total of what I said to Jo for six hours. Getting to our hotel in the city wasn't so different from any driving I'd done, but I was grateful her steering freed me to watch for the ocean. All that water was a curiosity.

"Cavalier on the Hill," I read out when we arrived. She pointed us between brick columns, gold words hanging on them. Joseph or not to guide us,

there were plenty of parking spaces. Choosing far
from the door since we had so little to carry, she act-
ed saintly, leaving white lines on asphalt for those
who are less fortunate. When Jo opened the car
trunk, the car's air conditioning had nearly frosted
my nubbly make-up case.

Inside the hotel, off the Cavalier hall that said
LOBBY, I wandered into one room with flowery
drapes throwing glints of sunshine right onto the
black-speckled floor. Jo cranked her neck to take in
the place. The dowdy white tennis shoes she wore
looked like separate saucers of cream on a fancy
kitchen counter. We tiptoed, appreciating water on
the pool level below shining like a blue mirror.
Padded wicker furniture and a glass-topped table
held a brown-streaked coffeepot beside dirty cups
and saucers, all of which was exactly like Victor and
Nikki's patio on *The Young and the Restless* (except
that Miguel, who's their male domestic, cleans that
show's mess up quicker).

Jo couldn't compare that indoor pool to anything
she watched on daytime TV. I could imagine me
along with Dwain's baby boy lounging near our
heart-shaped pool. A dream nanny would scoop up
the baby and then me and Dwain would slip in the

pool naked. I'd float while he kissed me everywhere, if he could dog paddle.

Jo, as usual, was practical. "Bring your suit, Rita?" she asked. I didn't even own one. "Cutoffs," I said. I don't trust the ocean for more than wading.

Jo spoke between gold cage bars to someone who slid a card across the lobby counter. She went ahead carrying that little card to our room, me trucking our clothes. When our room door swung open, we stepped onto odd carpeting, into space that smelled like Mike's office, lemony, suggesting no one had slept there before. We had a suite, each our own big bed and giant television separated by a folding flimsy door. I had a notion to get the Playboy channel late and didn't want her guessing. She sat for a while on the edge of her bed, me in an armchair off to the side. She unlaced her shoes, saying it was the time of an evening her feet began to swell.

When she finally moved, and I was restless at having to sit there and visit with her in a bedroom, Jo washed her face loudly in the slick black bathroom. I heard her run gushes of bathwater to disguise pee trickles, and slide the door on its track closed between us. Switching from Home and Garden TV, I learned that some people in taxicabs in Las Vegas will do anything, tell about it, show everything they have to strangers.

In the morning, and for the first time I remember, Sister Josephine direly needed my help. Fingering the meeting brochure, she headed to the bathroom in a long gown, came out dressed, combed, and holding her sad tennis shoes up to her caved-in chest. "We meet at 9, Rita. Guess you'll be ready?"

"Almost am," I said, pinching my white bra strap underneath narrow blue arches crossing my not-yet-suntanned shoulders. Dressed for anything, I was boiling energy inside the blue Hills tank top and white jeans. My outfit screamed summer at the beach, but it reassured my boss that I could be ladylike in public, banded as I was. An obvious bra strapped my scrawny boobs. Dwain, who could be complimentary and critical at the same time, usually wolf-whistled and said, "just a mouthful, enough for me." Since the pool dream from the night before, he had shriveled in my thoughts.

While I was no fashion plate, Jo was a sight. Big orange and gold loopy flowers on a skirt and top swirled and competed until her tightly-curled gray hair, plus equally-tight gray face, were lost.

Much as I didn't understand her, I'd had weeks to observe. Thinking for the first time from her side about risk she'd taken by accepting me over the summer, I decided to chance something myself. Also, I could show her a thing or two about what really interested me.

"Pale, Jo." Just that much I said, but her stick arms flew out to hug her flowered middle. I sort of guided her, and Jo sat up stiff on the end of my bed. She held her meeting canvas bag labeled *SOCIAL SERVICES, Fair for Everyone* balanced on top of clean tennis shoe laces. Getting pots and packets from inside my make-up case, I went to work.

"Don't use the green eye shadow," she said. "Too bright." That color was similar to the one they had locked up as shoplifting evidence on me, so I skipped it for blush and powder. I painted Plum Crazy on her thin lips, but I rubbed so hard to tone it down that the toilet paper rolled up in wormy shreds. I had cautioned her not to move while I brought out her soft blue eyes, the crinkles at the corners that deepened when she listened to every momma's story in Social Services. I was proud that she hadn't flinched, had trusted me when it mattered. A light spritz of Baby Soft Body Cologne, the label turned so she couldn't see, finished her. When she stood in front of the bathroom mirror, "If you think so," was all she said about her appearance.

Downstairs, at our meeting—and I was confident walking into a roomful of strangers with Jo looking so good—I grabbed two bran muffins and two cartons of juice from the table. I sat on a leather bench beside Jo as she chewed. She scanned her brochure, maybe trying to hide her new face until the lipstick wore off. "Meeting Room A," she said seriously when she stood up, smoothing her skirt in back.

"C," I said. Jo was okay as a chaperone, but I wanted to test if I could slip away. Forking down that hall, around the corner and past the knot of women clumped at the door, I made it outside toward the board sidewalk.

The ocean, when I finally saw it, was grander than I expected. Roaring and pounding sand, the wild water buoyed ships in the distance to float unbelievably still. Walking on the sugary stuff, I realized that standing on top of glare was amazing shit. Wiping grit from corners of my eyes, I tasted a finger that salt from the breeze powdered. I was thirstier than I thought for.

Five minutes later, plopping down on dry sand, I cuddled two cans of Pabst from the 7-Eleven I had picked out as soon as Jo drove into Virginia Beach. The first beer threatened to pop open inside a smooth

brown bag the clerk had handed me flat for just this
moment. A lot happier than I had been drinking free
orange juice, I counted four of my five dollars gone.
The first brew made a cheerful creek down my throat
as ocean waves stomped the shoreline so hard my
ears heard bellowing. The entire ruckus was louder
than when a Charolais bull in Bland gets separated
from his ladies. As soon as I smacked foam off an up-
per Plum Crazy lip, I reached into my canvas *Fair for
Everyone* bag to snag the cold second brew.

Cool refreshment under already-hot sun reminded
me of Dwain's vision of coolness. What he studied,
private in his thoughts while he and his brothers
roofed in frying ninety degree heat, was my white
cotton underpants. Dwain actually told me just that
on our first night in the cemetery.

Going together last year had been innocent, because all Dwain and I did each Friday was nibble a
double hamburger without onions in his front seat,
lick down not more than one shared beer, and neck
sitting up. Things got hot when I started work.
Maybe my being arrested, his courting a wicked girlfriend for the first time, agitated him, because he
drove us to the Maupin cemetery the weekend after
we graduated.

"It would mean a lot to me, something a man really likes," he said before he asked me to, before he quit talking for a while. Unzipping his bulky pants crotch for the first time, I touched and satisfied him. Of course, Dwain would have done me, except I had cramps. Gurgling deep in his throat when he said I had some real talent, he encouraged me to perfect a technique. All summer, I yearned for that humid darkness like it was his blue Future Farmers of America jacket, a welcome break from community service's dress code. I did fancy moves with my tongue tip unless he communicated he was too tired from loading shingle bales up a ladder.

Blocks from the Virginia Beach meeting, a carnival at the edge of the sand down the beach waved me over. Candy apple ladies dipped, arranging red globes on ledges at their booths. Italian sausage men chopped bushels of green peppers with cleavers they waved at one another, threatening people's balls. Cute boys polished kiddie car wheels; they had to let old ugly drunks press the buttons to guide the vehicles over tracks.

However the morning passed, it was too quickly 12:30. "Queasy," I said to Jo back at the meeting when I didn't get in an awful line to pick up my ham and cheese sandwich. They served lunch sandwiches in children's sand buckets, the plastic shovels making them lopsided to carry. Iced tea with extra sugar and four lemon slices disguised my beer breath until we went to the afternoon session, *Realizing Potential– Whether Customer or Staff*. In that one, Jo and I were partners for a work group. We drew the best blobs with captions, connected all the right lines. The instructor beamed, letting us go at 5 p.m., concluding we had got empowerment to last a year.

"Not really the best for my situation," I said truthfully when Jo asked about how my morning workshop had gone. She'd heard that all the sessions had lost attendees to the sunny beach. "Me among them," I said lightly, proud I could say the truth instead of a lie. I showed her the slight sunburn exactly at the edge of my straps, then offered to carry both our sets of handouts up to our room.

"Not yet," Jo said, pulling toward my morning route. She stood in a little dip of sand, those white shoes marking her, as gawky as an unusual sea bird. In addition, her make-up had worn off. Before I knew it, she had put the shoes in her canvas bag and was starting off barefoot. Jo yelled over the wind for me to follow her in the direction of the carnival I'd seen earlier.

I knew it was because she didn't get out much. Looking neither toward the Ferris wheel nor the heavy hammer-bell booth a snaky line of cute guys waited to do, she drew in front of a ball toss, eyeing blue teddy bears pegged as prizes. She dug for a dollar she didn't ask to be changed. She lost her money in four throws.

"Rigged, Jo," I said as I pulled her across scraggly grass toward food for sale. She got last in a long line to order us two barbecues with slaw, two large lemonades. Feeling bad about her clenching one drink's waxed cup in her teeth while she teetered with the cardboard carton holding everything else, I took her elbow and escorted her to a picnic table. As luck would have it, we ended up back of the Onion Garden. Before I got a good look at the back end of the business, a girl about my age with jet-black waist-length hair rushed out the back door of the onion booth. Dark eyes flooding tears, the girl sat down on the one step, hollering louder than most people call pigs.

How no one else noticed this drama was amazing. Laying our supper on the grass, we ran over and held her hands when she began yanking her hair, pounding a balled fist into her slim thigh. Over some little time, Jo figured out the story. Early afternoon, her father, who feared he was having a heart attack, left the booth for the city hospital. He was talking to her on the telephone just as we wandered by. No heart attack, he reported, but they couldn't rule out gall-bladder trouble. Doctors wanted him to keep motion-less on a narrow hospital bed until morning, when he could most likely get back to business. Gina, the daughter, had bushels of onions sectioned to batter. As always, she and her father had planned to fry golden flowers for hungry crowds as the midway heated up.

Jo suggested something immediately. "Let us in, Gina," Jo said, gesturing at the bottom half door locked between us and the interior Onion Garden.

"I can't trust the business to strangers," Gina said.

"My dad taught me." I guessed she feared we'd rob her.

"Jo's a Catholic sister," I said stupidly, probably the last thing my boss wanted told.

"Rita is crucial to my plan," Jo said. In a rush, I suspected Virginia Beach was educational in a way I hadn't guessed. We tied on checked aprons.

"I worked in a kitchen when I was in the convent," Jo said, all the credentials she needed. She traced the

spattered recipe card with her crooked first finger, measuring flour and cracking eggs for batter. I whisked water into the mess. She let me dip the first onion; I dripped batter everywhere. Getting her rhythm, she fried the onion flowers until they floated, petals pointy brown. Gina took customer orders, putting plastic cups of honey-mustard dip inside the center cutout as Jo drained onions. Underneath the cooking table managing the cashbox, I passed ones and bigger as Gina sang out what change she needed. For a while, the only people on the midway were teenagers who were too cool to eat.

"Take a break," Gina said. When Jo stepped out to get our abandoned lemonades, and Gina scooped ice to add to them from her machine, I made my move. In one second, when their backs turned, a ten-dollar bill from the cash box ironed itself flat in my thigh pocket as if no fingers had ever touched it.

From 11:30 until midnight, customers straggled as the rides speeded up. "Take your break without me," Jo said. "You haven't seen the carnival. All this hard work, and you're even better at it than you do make-up!"

At a diagonal from the Onion Garden, and out of Jo and Gina's sight in case I lost at a game of skill, I handed the blue teddy bear guy the ten I'd taken. I asked him for five in change, certain I could win Jo a stuffed bear with that little bit.

Figuring I could toss wild to bust balloons that looked level, I made a miscalculation. Bored with the spare crowd in front of his tent, raking money from me—loser like the rest—the guy began to fix on my cleavage. I jiggled on purpose when I pulled out the last five dollars from my pocket.

Bobbing a toothpick at one corner of his mouth, he sucked a front gold tooth in appreciation, creaking his bristly neck to gawk at my butt. "Too bad, baby," he said. Sweat ran steady down my neck. My money had almost vanished.

I thought how the big bear would tickle when the man whose shirt said *BILL* pushed the blue plush hide into my arms. I'd feel tall as the highest cloud when I walked beside Jo carrying the prize to the car. I couldn't wait to tell her I had won it for her. Another thing I could be good at in her eyes.

"Sure'd like me one of those," he said, squeezing his right thumb and forefinger together. It was his singular thought, generated from staring at my tit. "When you're fifteen," he croaked, heaping up nastiness.

"My Dwain'll kick your ass," I said as soon as I could. I twisted the ring around so the fake-silver showed a definite band. "I'm married to Dwain. We're 21; well, he is." My money credits had run out. The man began lowering a shade over the prizes, untouched blue bears snagging the bottom slat as the curtain fell.

"Take this then, baby," he said, turning toward me, holding the biggest blue animal I'd seen. "You need somebody to love you right."

It was like Jo with the Onion Garden, how soon I had a plan. Thanking him with a shy smile, I set the bear on the counter, its flat feet bottoms pointing straight out, round and fresh like newly-sawed pressure-treated post tops.

"Is that right? You a big stud?" I said.

"Not that you'll know."

"Well, I'll tell you what. When I get home I'm gonna have a problem. Dwain don't like me spending his roofing money for trash, and he'll see I'm down ten. Some way I could earn that amount of money back?"

"Let's us talk about that around back if you're old enough to take a drink of liquor. Now that we're closed," he said.

The man swung rickety lattice, letting me walk across plastic grass that his pointy-toed boots dented

not at all. We went in the back to a folding chair next to
a crate. A squarish bottle of Jack Daniels on top of slats
was the tallest thing. His boots planted that man, the
worst kind of weedy shrub, alongside the chair I sat in.

His plaid arm crooked for him to take a long drink,
and he wiped his mouth when he finished. Cleaning
the bottle lip with my tank top hem, I leaned forward
just a little so he could see down my shirt. I lapped a
burning dot of whiskey, all the while splashing and
churning the brown thin liquid inside glass.

"About that ten?" I asked when my eyes teared.

"For ten, sure," he said from where he stood beside
me. He rubbed his crotch mound across my cheek.
One hand fished around to his back pocket; he pulled
out my money he'd taken. Making a little show of
folding it as many times as I could, pleating the dirty
bill like a fine baby-dress yoke, I made his eyes pop
when I pushed the money between my breasts.

"Okay, get ready. I don't swallow. Not even Dwain."

Unzipping with his right hand, he pushed his left
thumb between my Plum Crazy lips, poking in a
metallic taste of quarters that set my teeth on edge.
Not that I could have done the violence to his man-
liness, but I bit down on that wide hang-nailed thumb
as hard as I possibly could. I kicked the folding chair,

with its considerable bruising potential, into his shins. The only one who saw me sprint back to Onion Garden was that stupid staring bear.

Jo had batter in her hair and all over her shirt, but she was wiping the counters in careful streaks. I opened my hands, palms up, and shrugged at her and Gina. "The carnival's better here," I said, "easier to be on the inside taking suckers' money."

"I'm disappointed for you, Rita," Jo said later as we pulled the grade, walking back to our hotel.

"I'm disappointed in me too, Jo," I said. "Everything's rigged."

"You'll have another chance," she said.

"I didn't have what it took for a game of skill OR chance," I said when I slammed the car trunk lid over our small bags.

"You missed something, Rita," Jo said. I thought she meant a suitcase or my Kroger sack I had forgotten to pick up.

"Now what's my fault?" I said. It sounded ugly, and too rough for Jo, but I was rotten and knew it.

"I said I'm disappointed FOR you, Rita," she said.

"But you heard I'm disappointed IN you. No matter what you think of Bland, and all the people around you, you're your biggest critic."

"Lay off," I said. "I don't work for you anymore. Like I ever did."

I rearranged our little packages, sadly flat and low on vacuumed trunk carpeting. They shone lavender under a yellow-green streetlight at the edge of the parking lot. All of a sudden, like a snake bit me in there, the effect I wanted, I yanked my hand out. I stared down at my left ring finger.

"Gone," I said, mortified. My eyes were slits to gauge her reaction.

"What?" Jo asked, touching my elbow closest to her gently, taking a step backward.

"Dwain's ring," I said in a trembly voice. Lying dripped off my lips. "You know… ," I said, rocking back and forth while I pretended to rethink the evening. "The first onion!" I said. "Bet the ring came off in the batter."

Because Jo was that kind of lady, we rushed back to Gina's onion booth. That grateful girl hadn't yet scraped the cold cream off her face, or put on pajamas, to get ready for bed. Gina ran for Kleenex to wipe the slick stuff off her nose so her glasses would stay put and she could see to help. I stared miserably around the buckled floor where we'd worked, then knelt to block the view, a white knee alongside the open cash box.

Quick as I could will it to happen, my hand dipped
into my bitty jeans change pocket and hooked out
the fake-silver 7-Eleven band I'd hid there. I pressed
the jewelry into the cloth covering one knee on the
floor, paining myself with the sensation of kneeling
on jacks. By the time I stood and the cheap ring
clinked to the floor in the hollow between my arches, I'd done what I intended.

"Good for you," Gina and Jo sang out. It had been
a group effort, and they hadn't caught on to my deceit.

Driving home through the inky night, sliding us
along the highway, Sister Jo let me keep my window
way down. I heard odd birds stirring out there along
the roadside.

"Virginia Beach wasn't so different from home," I
said. 'I thought I'd be scared."

"Why?" Jo said. "I knew you'd do just fine."

"It's different for you, Jo. You been exposed
to things."

"Rita," she said. "Doubts come from you, not
from Bland people or Dwain or even Marva's father,
the sheriff."

Jo had reason to trust me, and I felt justified about
my actions. The start was—and I replayed it often as
we rode—with my hand in Gina's cash box. Just like

a hero in a drive-in movie, I saw me lay that nasty
midway man's ten on top of the other bills at Gina's.
So when Jo commenced singing the words to unfamiliar hymns, I hummed right along.

Phil Gruis is a former editor of daily newspapers who spent most of the nineties in the Montana wilderness. He now lives and writes in Sandpoint, Idaho, and Johnson's Landing, British Columbia. His poems have been accepted by Bear Deluxe, Pontoon, Erosha *and* Poetry Motel.

Madman of Manito Place

BY PHIL GRUIS

Walking the dog this black lion
along park's edge
we are no distraction at all
to the queue of stately homes

harrumphing old gents
heads deep in broadleaves
who say through yawns
they've seen it all.

But yellowed eyes flicker
as a furious rant
sears the spring air.

A young wedge of a guy
on a veranda by a brick manse
howls that he will kill
that fucking bitch who
must have done him wrong
and the person with whom

she must have done it.

In throat-ripping screams
he recites the gory options.

Rage twists and burns his face
tautens his white T-shirt
flails his thick arms
stomps the flagstone.

All along the dappled street
old gents anxious now enfold
in brick and oak
frail homebodies
who cower in their gauzy rooms

yearning for gunshots sirens
SWAT teams yellow tape TV crews
a tale deliciously new
should they live to tell it.

So maybe she shredded his heart
laughed at his dick
ran off with a pool cleaner.

PHIL GRUIS

Or it's about the Jag
he couldn't get
or maybe within him blazes
some other fierce want
of the kind that wealth begets.

I could kill you
he screams over azaleas
at me and the prancing dog.

I turn to show him my back
which once
like his
was straight and strong
knowing that when it was
I would have roared
come on motherfucker.

Marjorie Maddox, Director of Creative Writing and professor of English at Lock Haven University, has published Transplant Transport, Transubstantiation *(Yellowglen Book Prize, WordTech, 04),* Perpendicular As I *(Sandstone Book Award, 1994), five chapbooks, and over 270 poems, stories, and essays in literary journals and anthologies. She is the co-editor of* Common Wealth: Contemporary Poets on Pennsylvania *(forthcoming from PSU press, 2005).*

Crowned

BY MAJORIE MADDOX

Pumpkin, apple, sorghum, blueberry—I do all the festivals. Judge giant pies the size of wading pools. Win goldfish religiously. Sip milkshakes as thick as all my wishes. At each one, I am the queen, a half-wave to the left, a half-wave to the right, riding on a shiny John Deere or a customized Cadillac while my court follows on Harleys or streamered pick-ups. What does the rest of my life matter when I have a basket of berries; when 4-H kids stand on their tip-toes and point at my crown?

You don't have to be television-pretty. I am the preacher's kid and have 23 freckles on my face, one for each of my talents, my daddy says. I think it's for the times we'll move, in and out of duplexes, refurbished garages, a parsonage in need of electricity and paint. We arrive well before the voting, when any new girl is cute enough, and a minister's someone important, his wife voted to every committee.

But there's only Daddy and I and the empty slots for Dog Sled or Quilting Festival Queen. My hair is long, shiny, uncut. Daddy says that's the crown of any girl, that and a Christian-way-of-being, honest-like and full of thank-you's. I catch on quick, remember how Mama was before the baby that took them both. It wasn't Jesus that did it. He let his Mama live. Saved her one of the biggest crowns in heaven. My Mama has one too, I'm sure, sparkled as sweetness. But I don't think the baby's there, seeing what she did by trying to be born too quickly. She should have waited her turn.

Daddy and I know about taking turns. When he sees someone at the convenience store, scowling as he sorts through the Shop Mart guides, Daddy says to me, "This one is yours. Turn on that pretty smile and tell him about Jesus." When he sees a new bank teller or the secretary at the town insurance company, he says, "This one is mine" and smiles big as eternity. Then he gives her directions to church and our number. We know what's to be done. If you're not nice, there's nobody to fill the pews. It's the job, and we work quickly. "There's only so many days before Jesus comes back," Daddy says each time he sees a new clerk at the Coastal Mart.

Time keeps moving and people move with it. Knowing that makes it easy. People will wave good-bye in a few months anyway no matter what. The first Sunday they return all our smiles. The next Sunday too. The next months, their fuses fizz away a bit more each time they shut the church door, walk back to their own lives. I know because of what my daddy knows: how their pity reminds them of their own pain, and their pain embarrasses them.

At first, they bring Daddy's favorite casseroles, though I cook just fine. Next, they bring stories of their mothers, their own losses, hidden inside bites of upside-down cake. Finally, they forget about us and our lives. They want us to forget about theirs. They look away, trying to erase their calls at midnight, their shaky voices, the lives they don't put on parade. I watch them during my solos of "When the Saints Come Marching In." By the last notes, they don't remember my festival crown. They see instead my father's eyes, the slant of his nose, remember the words he's heard.

I hear some of them too, though I'm not supposed to. What can I do when Sally Moore's mother arrives red-eyed on the doorstep, a bruise tattooing her arm? She needs my daddy to listen, so I go for the ice. Her words heave between the chorus of sobs. "It's only sometimes," she says, her voice not believing itself. When my daddy's strong arm goes around her, she calms a bit, but keeps talking. Her life comes out of her lips: how her own daddy was, where she'd lived. She was even a festival queen like me, but only once. My own breath comes fast as I wait for her to finish the hard part. She says what has been stuck inside too long: the way she got the baby before she should have. How she married quick, without even a proper dress or a daddy who would give her away. It's then my daddy whispers Bible verses in her ear, the way he did to me when I was a little girl. When I look down, the ice is dripping tiny puddles at my feet. I let it dry up by itself and head to the bedroom.

The next week the plant closes and Bob Harker sobs on Daddy's shoulder right in the middle of the hardware store. I have the basket with all the stuff we're buying: a new roll of screen for the backdoor to keep the flies out, more oil for the squeaky door hinge that wakes me up each time Daddy has to go out at night. Standing in line with some rope, Mr. Harker sees Daddy and his eyes well up. Then the crying starts. Loud. Even Julie, the cash register girl, knows to look away. Daddy takes him by the shoulder and walks him over by the electric saws where no one else is. They're gone long enough for me to go up and down most of the aisles three times. Then I just sit up front by the Child Safety display and work on my memory verses. When I get done with that, I practice my festival speech, quiet-like so no one can hear. I even practice the hand gestures, imagining the audience. At the end, I look up, thinking how light the new crown will feel.

It's almost closing time when Daddy and Mr. Harker come out. The rope's gone. Instead, Daddy's got us a new Welcome Mat and holds it up to show me. He shakes Mr. Harker's hand, as if nothing's happened. Says he'll see him at church.

We're a team like that, Daddy and I. We're the $1 + 1 = 2$ for Noah's ark. We're a right foot and a left foot to march around Jericho. We're the hands to pick the wheat for the holy harvest. So when Freddy Schmidt smashes the family car into the front of Greeley's Garage six hours before Sunday School, we both go. It's just across the street and down a bit, and the ambulance sirens blast through the walls of our tiny house and into the one bedroom. Daddy's up first, tugging on some shorts and a WWJD T-shirt. Quick, like that, then he's out the door. I'm right behind him with some shorts over my nightie. No time for a bra.

When we get there, the ambulance guys are prying Freddy out of the Buick. He's dazed and bleeding across his forehead, Jesus-style. The garage store-front is a mess. Glass everywhere. The car is propped up like those modern sculptures they have at the museums, the front end smashed in like a flattened milk carton. One tire is still spinning. A poster that reads: "Change Your Oil. It's Sooner Than You Think" hangs crookedly from what's left of the one wall. There's no alarm, this being a small town, but the neighbors have all come out and stare at the wreck from across the street. They're comparing raising-kid stories, I think. Daddy waves at them, then holds his praying hands up high. The ambulance lights flash across his fingers. It's then I think Freddy looks at me, just for a second, smiling as they carry him off on the stretcher.

We get to the hospital even before his parents, and Daddy puts me on door watch. It's only a few minutes before the Schmidts come rounding the corner in the other car, the one mostly she uses, a rusted-out Toyota. Mr. Schmidt is driving too fast (who wouldn't?), but the parking lot is pretty empty so there's lots of space to make up for the bad turns and the speed. He parks crooked, taking up two spaces, and they're out and running in. She's got on a nightgown and shorts like I do; he's dressed like Daddy, but with a Harley T-shirt. They almost don't see me, but I know enough to run with them, pointing toward a doctor and Daddy. Just like on TV, only better. My daddy's there for Mrs. Schmidt to wrap her arms around. She's crying hysterically and even reaches for my hand twice. It's a good morning, considering. Freddy ends up okay, and Daddy takes me out to Perkins before Sunday School. I get hash browns, pancakes, and scrambled eggs. The waitress recognizes me from my picture in the paper.

In every town, that's how it starts. In the next weeks, grateful choruses of *Amen's* will punctuate the sermons. They'll be Sunday supper invitations, strong hand shakes and kisses on the cheek. Then the spaces between, the shopping lists jotted on the back of bulletins, the kids-have-a-cold excuses, the rushed good-byes. After that, the complaints: sermons too long, budget too high, attendance too low, building too cold.

So before all that, I try to remember the parades. I hold the day in my head like a prayer, deeply inhale the peanut/greasy fries/caramel apple smell that circles everyone in town, halo-style. I look and see the not-yet familiar faces, un-scrubbed for Sunday but breaking with the same other-worldliness that hymns give, a sudden note of joy that takes you from a job you hate and lets you breathe in and out without thinking. The kids are happy and kiss their mothers. The parents hold hands. Most of them recognize me and wave. Like my daddy, I am up front, where everybody looks. I think my crown shimmers like the heavenly ones.

It's the same in every town, wherever we go. The parade rides down whatever the largest street is, past whatever church has hired Daddy, and up toward some rented Ferris wheel, where chips of rust float like confetti out over the game barkers. Someone will offer to win me a giant teddy bear or a new Bible, but I'll be listening to the marching band's last song—brash and off-key—the town fire engines shrieking their sirens, prophesying, as I do, what is coming. Because I know.

Daddy says talent is God-given, but I know it's just memorizing the patterns, the important dates, the order and kinds of parades, and what to do when it rains. I can sing and dance okay. I can ride a unicycle without breaking my leg. I can even do three back flips in a row, but that's not what wins me my crown. I know what people want by looking at them.

I know who will let out the pain, who will want someone else to feel it. They see a motherless girl and they think, "She knows." They see a man without a wife, and they think, "He knows." It's in their eyes, just when they finish smiling hello. It's in what's left of their voices after they shake hands. Like an aftertaste that won't go away. That's how it was with Miss Samuels, even before she brought the pies wrapped up with a ribbon.

And the others, the ones who already have kids, they think I am more grateful than their own children. Maybe I am. I have less time and take what I can. I sing "Danny Boy" for Mrs. McCleary, recite the twenty-third Psalm for Joe Johnston, tap-dance "Yankee Doodle Dandy" for old Mr. Abernathy. "What a lovely girl," they say, then listen closely to my daddy's sermons, his voice too kind for any carnival boy hawking frozen bananas.

I want them to listen, but not closely. Not enough to repent. When they repent, they only do so halfheartedly, even when they mean it at the time. They walk down that aisle at the altar call and want to be different. When they walk back, they think they are. When they walk out the big double doors, a little wears off, but not much. When they walk back for

Wednesday service, they're sure they've got it down, but then they hear Daddy's soft voice. They remember something they didn't do that they should have or something they shouldn't have done that they did, and they walk down the aisle again. The next week it's a little harder and a little harder still after that.

By the time five Sundays have passed, Mrs. Moore has another bruise, only this time just her eyes say something. Part of what they say is shame. Her husband is an elder. They always are. His eyes say embarrassed. They say, forget what you know.

That's what my eyes used to say every time the congregation decided we knew too much. What the people told us was different: they didn't have enough to pay, or Daddy's sermons weren't good enough, or they got a full-time pastor, one with a wife and five girls, all pretty. These days, my eyes aren't embarrassed. There's always another town, another festival, another parade with unfamiliar faces. At least that's what I tell myself each night when I'm supposed to be saying my prayers.

This month it's Millville and the Strawberry Festival. The people have different names, but inside they're mostly the same. We arrive on a Thursday in May—after the Coal Festival in Blossburg, before the

Corn Festival in wherever we end up next. By the next Tuesday, after Daddy's sweet-voice sermon and my solo on Sunday, I am nominated and out back of the Town Hall being questioned by the judges. It's the first thing in the morning. My freckles are a plus. In the sun, my hair looks a little red, so I'm a natural for the part. The church is a festival sponsor, though most of its girls are too young or too old. Wholesome is what this group wants, a good example for its youth.

After a dozen or so towns, I know the part. I wear a hand-sewn blouse from the last town's ladies' circle, sky blue the color of innocence with a large strawberry for each collar. The shirt flattens my breasts and falls halfway down my calf-length skirt. It's the right choice. I quote a poem from a Hallmark Mother's Day card. Then, to the tune of "We Are Gathered Together," I trill a song about the town. It's a quick revision to what I performed four towns back. I hold out the last notes long and loud then smile with all my teeth. The men look at their wives for their reactions. The women nod approvingly.

When the first weekend in June rolls around, Daddy is still the man up front in the pulpit. I am still the new festival queen. We are riding high, getting ready for my crown. Three new families have joined the church. The offering is up. Crops are good. We've had supper invitations each week, twice from Miss Samuels, who, she reminds us again though we don't need telling, makes the best pies in town.

Daddy is preaching on the fruits of the spirit, and the older ladies are trying to identify who has what gift. Three of the younger girls are my court; they smile like junior bridesmaids and wear their hair like mine, a braid twirled into a loose bun, like a hat slipped to the back of the head. One of the girls' grandmother makes us matching red-gingham dresses with a sash the color of vines.

In the parade, we're up front, where we should be. This time, Daddy, the girls, and I all ride in the same car, a convertible, maroon Thunderbird from Walter's backyard mechanic shop. One of the doors is blue and rusting. There are crepe-paper leaves draped across the sides. The girls are scrunched together in the back like triplets, and I ride up front with Daddy, who turns the key as if he's young again and heading out on his honeymoon. My winner's banner is tight and, because it's hot, the ribbon sticks a bit at my shoulder. The *S* in Strawberry Queen is partly gone and looks like a backwards *c*. I don't mind.

I've clipped the gold-sprayed crown in place with bobby pins, but if I wave too vigorously, it tips a bit, back and forth. I try to keep my head straight, yet there's too much to see. The booths are lined up outside the church and down the street: strawberry ice cream, strawberry shortcake, strawberry cupcakes in ice-cream cones, strawberry pudding, strawberry soda, strawberry crepes. There's a booth for weaving strawberry placemats and one selling strawberry air freshener. A woman on the corner, not a churchgoer, holds up strawberry pinwheels and lets them spin in the wind.

Daddy drives us past slowly. I breathe in the redness, pick out faces in the crowded patch of near-strangers. Then there are the others, the ones who've told us too much. They wave, too.

The high school band blasts "In the Good Old Summertime," hold their heads high, and bounce their knees up to their chests. Just behind us, six- and seven-year-olds, dressed like strawberries, do cartwheels and flips for the clapping bystanders. It's time for me to throw candy, so I reach in one of my baskets and pull out strawberry taffy, each piece attached to a pink curl of paper with a different fruit of the spirit and a Bible reference penned in neat calligraphy. A crowned missionary, I'm spreading the Word!

Then Daddy turns the wheel and heads us to the town square, where a merry-go-round twirls its fantasy promises in the middle of a large circle of park benches. I want doves, but they've flown away. A few sparrows twitter in their place, trying to keep tune with the pretend ponies. At the stand next to the strawberry fritters, past the Tunnel of Love and Monster's Scare Shack, Miss Samuels stands outside her red-checkered booth, her pies stacked neatly inside, away from the heat. Her sign is in large, curvy calligraphy, but she's standing so I can't see the price. A single spot of strawberry filling dots her lower lip. When she looks at my daddy, her eyes hold the light, the same way the candles shine in them during Holy Communion. And she is waiting to tell him her life.

I start singing "A Bicycle Built for Two" for my daddy, so he'll look at me instead, but it's too late. He is already waving at Miss Samuels, his left hand high in the air. He forgets he's a preacher. By the time he glances toward me, he's at the corner and takes the turn—even at slow speed—a bit too sharply, just enough so the girls in back say, "Whoa!" The car nudges up against the curb, and I have to steady my crown. When he looks again at me, his face is different. His eyes are a question. For a moment, I forget the sound of his voice. Without his striped tie and white shirt, he's just a regular dad, so I keep my face ahead and smile, looking toward the horizon where I'm sure the next town is hiding, ready to be found, like a strawberry too long in the sun.

J. O'Nym is a bass player. Her poems have appeared in many journals and anthologies, including Calyx *and* Borderlands *and has work forthcoming in* Hanging Loose. *She has co-written songs with Meg Hentges on the albums* Tattoo Urge, Afterlaugh, *and* Brompton's Cocktail *and is working on a new recording,* E Cat *for the band Skidding Kitty. She was the recipient of a poetry fellowship from the Texas Writers' League in 2003.*

In 1964

BY J. O'NYM

The sixties were like that, filled with dangerous
    toys and ideas—
I stood on the hump in the back seat of my
    father's black Catalina convertible, seat belts
    stuffed down into the crack, as we wheeled
    around corners,
flew through the night to white suburbia, 90 mph
    to the coming decades,
not one thought to consequence.

When our father was drunk, our mother brought
    dangerous elements
into the house for us to play with—when the floors
    were waxed
to a high-gloss sheen, we took out the bottle of
    mercury she bought
from the pharmacist, poured out a puddle apiece,
    smashed them
with our thumbs, sent shiny balls scattering across
    the smooth surface of tile, then herded them

back together into a melded shimmer, liquefied
poison absorbed into our skin, along with the
notion that if we were not like
our father, we would be immune to chemical
interruption.

Lisa Toboz earned an MFA from the University of Pittsburgh. Formerly a business manger at Pittsburgh City Paper, *she is teaching English in Osijek, Croatia.*

Road to Happiness

BY LISA TOBOZ

Five hundred bucks in my savings, fifty dollars a lesson. I told my instructor in the first lesson that I had to pass this test in ten.

"My boyfriend Ethan wants me to learn to drive so that I can visit him in Buffalo."

My instructor is Dave. He rolls his sleeves to his elbows, then jots notes on a clipboard. This is my second lesson, and he wants me to pull out of the parking space and into traffic. This is easy for most people, but I am afraid to drive. I am afraid I won't have enough control of the wheel, of swerving into the left lane, into oncoming cars.

"That's odd," Dave says. "Most people are afraid of driving too far over to the right."

I look at my hands on the wheel. I read once how easy it is for people to isolate themselves from the world by staying in the confinements of their cars. The thought of being cut off from the rest of the world even more than I already am makes me anxious.

I look over to Dave to get the go ahead. He is tapping his pen to his chin as if he is somewhere other than our lesson. He catches me looking at him, smiles and adjusts his tie. He is one of those ageless men who could be either 25 or forty, with a jagged scar like a lightening bolt above his left eye. *Battle scar*, he joked back at the office, when he caught me staring at it, fascinated. I tried not to connect the scar to driving.

"Why don't we drive down the hill, past the high school," he says.

The wheel is stiff and my arms are stiff and my shoulders feel as if they're going to collapse. I wonder if this is a side effect of my withdrawal, or general tension. I wonder how much of my medication is still left in me.

The high school reminds me of when my father tried to teach me to drive four years ago, when I was sixteen. It was a disaster. I couldn't coordinate glancing in the rearview mirror while keeping my eyes on the road. All of it, while trying to tune out his bitching.

"I know what I'm doing," I say, braking at a red light.

"I believe you, doll," Dave says. He smiles, not looking anything like my father. I watch him turn on the radio and tap the dashboard to the music, and then he reminds me that the light is green. We go.

I had been on Prozac for two years and stopped taking it about two weeks ago. It had become part of a routine, like washing hair and brushing teeth. Forty milligrams seven times a week. Pop one down before a piece of toast and dash out the door. I didn't feel that heaviness in my head anymore, like before Prozac, when I'd climb out of bed every other morning and stay in my pajamas until late afternoon. Around dinnertime, I would put on the same clothes I had worn throughout the week, walk to the store, buy a bag of Doritos, go home to shitty TV, and sink into myself.

After my parents' divorce, my sister moved across town with my mother, and I stayed with my father. We decided this would be the better way, so no one's feelings would be hurt. In my first days with my father, I shuffled quietly around the house, around the new wife, trying not to crinkle the plastic covering her furniture. I didn't want to be a burden in their house, stir the dust in this new life my father had created. I didn't know how long I could keep up the appearance that everything was just swell. It left me feeling asthmatic.

When my sister finally got her license, she'd call me up from our mum's, wanting to take me for a ride. She figured she'd be my ticket to freedom (it was hers, eventually, and that's how she got to Florida). All I could think about was the speed of cars; how I had read they are the most dangerous mode of transportation. I'd tell her no thanks, I'm afraid to die.

All I could think about were the car crashes I'd see on the news. Pile-ups and whole families crushed under metal. I made up stories about them in my head. The father lost his job and couldn't provide for his wife or little girl. He drove in front of a train and prayed, waiting for it to be all over.

During my fourth lesson, Dave asks me to drive figure eights around poles in a K-Mart parking lot. I find this to be therapeutic—the smoothness of the pavement, the steering wheel sliding through my hands as I turn.

"Doing great," he says. "Pretty soon, you'll be driving one of these babies yourself." He pats the dashboard, settles back in his seat. He loosens his tie. His arm is hanging out the window. Like Sunday driving: the radio turned to mid-blast, the wind in my hair, people strolling to their cars fresh from a blue-light special.

Dave leans forward and asks me to do the figure eights in reverse.

The wheel becomes slippery beneath my palms. "So that means I have to keep turning around, then, checking the rearview mirror?"

Dave laughs. "That would be the safe thing."

I pause for a long time as the engine revs. I shift to reverse. I'm shaky and nervous and suddenly, doing these turns backwards makes me feel like my life before my bottled happiness.

I am not doing figure eights. I am going in circles.

Ethan is the one who pressed the issue of getting my driver's license. He goes to school in Buffalo, and the long distance was getting harder to manage for us. We met a year ago, at the South Shore, where I waited tables. My eyes were red from crying that morning after a fight with my father. Ethan watched me from behind his newspaper, smiling when I'd walk past his table. He slipped me a note on a piece of napkin: *Call, if you want to talk. I'm always willing to listen.*

Don't you want the freedom of driving? He'd ask. You can visit me whenever you want, instead of relying on the bus. You could go wherever you want and never go back.

True, I tell him. But I like the long rides from Pittsburgh to Buffalo because I get to read, and even if I did drive, there's no way I'd drive that far alone.

The last time I rode anywhere alone was on a plane to Phoenix. A woman sat next to me. The skin on her face pulled tight across her cheekbones. Her features slumped near her ears. Her mouth seemed to be holding her nose, her cheeks, and her eyes all together. Where her left eye should have been was just a space for the eye, red and crescent-shaped as if someone took a knife and carved a half-moon in her brow bone. I strained to listen to her talk. Her words tumbled through her teeth.

Years later in Buffalo, Ethan and I lay twisted in sheets. "If you got your license, you wouldn't have to talk to freaks on the bus," he said, after I had told him about the woman on the plane.

"But I met that woman on a plane," I reminded him. "I felt so bad for her."

"Baby," he said, "you have to learn not to care about everything so much." He ran his fingers through my bobbed red hair.

"I know," I said. My chest tightened. "I can't help feeling bad for other people."

"You should grow your hair long," he said. He touched my shoulder. "Long hair is much more feminine."

I lifted my head to look into his face, to see if he was joking. He tapped me on the nose. I rested my head on his chest again. I calculated how long it would take for my hair to grow three more inches. I thought if I learned to drive, I would go to see my sister at Christmas. The loneliness of the sea in winter, my gift.

I was first aware of my depression on my trip to Phoenix. I was fifteen, and I flew there alone. My parents thought a vacation with my aunt would be good for me, after the divorce. Before the flight, in the airport, my mother made such a fuss about flying. She made me wear a sticker on the front of my overalls: *Hello, my name is.* She insisted the plane would crash into the ocean. But there is no ocean. I'll be flying over the Midwest. *One can never trust those pilots*, my mother said.

I liked watching the checkered plots of land move beneath me. Perfectly lined rows of houses, with pools in backyards next to wheat fields the color of sand. In Pittsburgh, hills twisted, roads started then stopped, leading you into cul de sacs, where the next neighborhood began if you stepped through the weeds. You could never see your neighbors.

As I watched scenes shift beneath me, the plane hit an air pocket and took a small dip. It made my stomach drop. I searched for clues from the other passengers, a sign that would tell me if we'd crash. A man snored beneath his newspaper. The woman with the smeared features watched the movie.

What do people think of right before they die? Their faces didn't tell me. I sat with my hands clenched in my lap, watching the land below.

The geography shifted as we reached the Southwest. Checkered plots turned into red and brown mountains and earth. When the plane landed, my head swelled with loneliness. It thumped with the plane along the runway. I longed for the green hills of home instead of Phoenix, with its homes of terra cotta roofs and back-to-back shopping centers. Endless strips of Dennys and Jack in the Boxes. The open space made me feel as if everyone could see everything inside of me.

All the homes in my aunt's complex looked the same. Pink stucco houses, with prickly pear cactus in the center of yards. Dirt yards and blue sky. I watched a group of Mexican boys at the car wash across the street, waxing the hoods of cars. They glistened and laughed and snapped towels at one another. I imagined one of them running his tongue along my teeth.

I watched talk shows all morning to avoid the brightness. The brightness cooked the pavement, skinning my feet when I walked to the pool. The sun made me feel guilty, reminding me that a beautiful day required attention and energy.

I wrote my sister a postcard a day. *Being here is like those dreams when you're running and you don't get anywhere.* By noon, I'd lie on a towel on my stomach, trailing my arm through the water.

My back burned. Tiny lizards crawled into my shoes. I felt as if I was in another world, as if I had crawled out of my skin and into someone else's. I turned onto my back, defying my pale skin, my loneliness, thinking of one of the boys at the car wash, running his hands across my head. Imagined him holding my heavy heart in his arms. I let myself bake in the sun.

In my sixth lesson we're zipping along the parkway. The speedometer reads 65, creeping toward seventy. The city disappears in the rearview mirror.

"Slow down there," Dave says, pressing his foot on the extra pedal on his side of the car. "I don't care how fast you go, but cops will."

I roll my eyes. I would think the freedom of this driving is wonderful, except I am too conscious of Kaufmann's Driver's Training painted on the side of the car. I click the left turn signal to switch lanes before I head through a tunnel. Dave is beaming; I have remembered what he has taught me. I grip the wheel more tightly, noticing that my hands are shaking. It has been almost a month since I've stopped taking my Prozac.

I'm getting low on the cash, and now it may come down to dropping the lessons or giving up therapy. I quit the South Shore because I was sick of dealing with people. I quit school because I couldn't concentrate long enough to study. I've applied for office work, the library. I realize that it's difficult to avoid the people issue. My father wants me to skip school, try to find a rich man to take care of me. I think of marriage as a prison sentence with no possibility for parole. Maybe I could file reports in a lawyer's office. Maybe I could become a film projectionist. I sometimes lay in bed at night, making sure I remember how to breathe.

I'm also nervous about being jobless because I have to pay what the insurance doesn't for my doctor visits. My father refuses to foot the co-pay. He doesn't believe in psychiatry. If you're going to be crazy, do it at your own expense. *Ha ha*, he says as I sit across from him at dinner. I look to my stepmother for some understanding. She shrugs. I stab a baked potato, shove the white softness into my mouth.

He loves to eat, my father. But he can go for an entire day without anything but water. Like those road trips he used to give my sister and me when we were little. Those eight hour trips to Chincoteague Island, when my parents were still married, when he drove down there without once stopping to let any of us pee. And when we finally got there, we scouted the island for two more hours, my sister and I pressing pudgy hands to the window, watching the wild ponies on the sides of roads chewing poison ivy slowly and evenly. He looked for bargains in motels, rooms that had beds with sand in the sheets and quilts with seashells printed on them. And after eleven hours of Kool Aid and pretzels, we fought to sleep, our stomachs rumbling in our dreams.

By the seventh lesson, Dave wants me to try parallel parking. He feels my driving abilities have progressed rapidly. These are his words. He sets up orange cones next to a curb on a small side street near my house, the same street where Ethan and I had sex in someone's back yard, standing against an above-ground pool when he was visiting. I wonder how I had the energy to do something like that.

"Remember," Dave says. He clasps his hands together and looks into the car. "Check the rearview mirror to see if anyone's behind you. Check your side mirror. Put it in reverse, then crank that baby into the space. You got it?" He sees me staring at the dashboard, my mouth hanging a little open. "You okay?"

I nod and breathe heavily.

Dave squats next to the driver's side, and rests his arms on the door, looking into the car. He rubs his eyes. His thumb slides over the scar above his eye.

"My mother taught me to drive when I was fifteen. We'd take the car in school parking lots, drive the figure eights, the three-point turns. And when it got to parallel parking, I was so frustrated because I was afraid I'd hit the car behind me. Or in front of me. And worried about my old man at home, threatening to wring my neck if I didn't know how to park blindfolded with one hand after one lesson."

I nod in understanding.

"She gave me the best piece of advice. She said, 'David, don't take life so damn seriously. You won't get out of it alive.'" He laughs. "That's from Bugs Bunny. She stole all her best advice from cartoons."

I laugh too, though death is the last thing I want to hear about.

I pull up so the tail end of the car aligns with the first cone. I try to imagine the two cars framing these cones. I glance in the rear view mirror. I check in the side mirror. I look at Dave because I already forget his instructions. I don't know how to ask him for help. I don't know what to do next.

I decide to buy Ethan a present. I feel guilty because I haven't told him about me going off the Prozac. It was his idea, and I don't want him to know that I actually considered his advice. Even though I'm helping myself, when you really get down to it.

I can't stand still enough to wait for a bus. I walk down Carson Street, to Tenth Street, and over the bridge. The wind kicks at my coat, blows hair into my mouth. Someone is walking behind me. Now he walks next to me. He's an old man, balding and snif-fling, with his hands shoved in his pockets.

"How are you today, pretty lady?"

"Fine." I look ahead.

"A little chilly today?"

"Yes."

"Long way to the other side, Red." He laughs, reaching out to touch my hair. I duck away from him.

The bridge seems to stretch for another mile.

"Are those pantyhose or tights you're wearing?" He stops laughing. His arm brushes against mine. I start to panic. Cars drive past, disappearing into the tunnel at the end of the bridge. I think of mouths, opening, closing, opening. I walk faster and he walks faster. "I wanted to know," he says, "because when I tie up my girlfriend, I use pantyhose."

He stands in front of me, blocking the wind and the view of the tunnel. He pulls from his pocket a picture of a girl, naked from the waist up, with what looks like a plastic bag covering her face. Her hands are tied above her head. It's an instant Polaroid. I can't stop looking at the picture. She could be bound and gagged in his basement. I push him out of my way as hard as I can. I turn around to go home. He follows.

"Get the hell away from me," I say. I shove my hands in my pockets to stop the tremors.

"I'm sorry," he says.

"Go to hell," I say.

"Clearly I've upset you," he says with concern in his voice. "You're too young to look so unhappy."

I'm surprised to hear that unhappiness is detectable, that it can be seen in a face. My face. I wonder how a man like this knows happiness.

I run ahead of him. I pause and look back, to make sure I've lost him. He is standing in the middle of the bridge. He waves to me.

"Have a nice day," he shouts. "Remember that picture I showed you."

He waves as if he's saying good-bye to an old lover. I run.

I run home and call Ethan at school in Buffalo and tell him about the man on the bridge.

"I'm calling the police. He could be stalking me."

"I told you not to walk over that bridge by yourself," Ethan says. "He's just some weirdo who walks around scaring young women."

"But that picture, Ethan—you didn't see that woman. It wasn't from some magazine, it was fucking real."

Ethan sighs into the phone, as if he trying to gather his patience. "He could have found it in one of the porn shops on the boulevard. Read a book or something to get your mind off things."

I'm suddenly angry that Ethan is four hours away, and I'm here and I can't stop the tremors in my hands.

"Easy for you to say, you aren't here to live this kind of shit."

"Will you stop being so overdramatic?" He sighs. "Did you talk to your doctor?"

"About the man on the bridge?" I say.

"About the pills. I think the pills are making you crazy."

"I'll work on it," I say.

I don't want to tell him because I like the power of knowing that I've gone off it without his hand-holding. I think of the first time my shrink wrote the prescription, the satisfied little smile on his face when he handed it to me. *You've made a good decision. You're on the road to a happier life.*

I twist the phone cord with my fingers. I think about the bottle of unopened pills in the bathroom cabinet. I laugh, because he doesn't know that this is me, without the drugs. I laugh because he is asking me what do I find so amusing. I can't stop my brain from racing.

In my eighth lesson, Dave wants to review what I've learned. "But first," he says, "I have something for you."

He reaches into his pocket. I close my eyes. After the bridge incident, I'm afraid to see. When I open them there is an electric blue rabbit's foot dangling in front of my face. I laugh.

"Thanks," I say, pinching it by the chain. "For luck."

"Bugs Bunny," Dave says. He winks.

I want to reach over and squeeze Dave's arm, but reconsider. It might be crossing the teacher-student boundaries. I run the rabbit's paw along my cheek.

"What did your dad do when you passed your driver's test?" I say.

Dave is jotting some notes on the clipboard. I look over to see what he is always writing about in our sessions. He covers the notes with his arm.

"He told me, now go down to Mellinger's and get me a case of beer." The scar above his left eye goes up in surprise. "I haven't thought about that in years," he says.

I want to laugh because I understand. I look over to see if Dave is laughing. He is making a list of all the things we have to review today: three point turns, the evils of parallel parking. I smile at him, but he is not looking at me. I slip the rabbit's paw into my pocket.

It is October, a month since I've taken my Prozac. Side effects of the withdrawal slip through the strongest when I dream. I'm half-awake. I think in fragments. The man on the bridge with his shining bald head. The woman in the picture. Her face covered. Or was her face smeared? Features mangled, all tumbled together like the woman on the plane.

I told my shrink about these dreams in one of our sessions. He said he was afraid I was slipping into another depressive episode. I feel as if I'm always trying to justify why I'm depressed. People want answers, and all you can give them are the feelings. I could say it is the divorce, a shitty home life. I could say that it's from living inside of my head too much. *Depression is anger turned inward.* What I know, I want to tell these people who ask, is that it's the general feeling that everything feels like nothing at all. I reach for ways to feel something, even if it's fear. Something to remind me that I'm still alive.

I write letters in my head to my sister, letters I don't have the energy to write down. Letters I'm afraid to say out loud because she will suspect that I may always be crazy: *I'm learning to drive. I need to find a job. I learned on* Jeopardy *that a person has a greater chance of being struck by lightening than winning the lottery. This gets me up in the mornings.*

A few weeks after the bridge incident, Ethan drives down from Buffalo. He pulls up in front of the house with a handful of daisies. There are leaves sticking to the bottoms of his shoes. He trails them into the house. We stand in the door, and he leans in to kiss me on the cheek, happy because I finally told him I went off the Prozac. *Ta-da! It's me*, I said over the phone, and did a tap dance he couldn't see.

My father and stepmother are at work. The first thing we do is tear off each other's clothes and have sex in the living room with the curtains open. Ethan likes the possibility of someone peaking in on us. I'd rather do it romantic-style on a bed in the dark, but I'm too tired to argue with him, so I give in.

When we finish, he is hungry. But first he goes to the bathroom to pee. He comes back into the living room, holding up my Prozac reserve.

"I thought you weren't taking this anymore?" He pinches his eyebrows together, examining the bottle.

"I'm not." I say. I close my eyes. I am lying on the floor naked, with my hands resting on my stomach. I feel a calm come over me. The shaking in my hands has lessened over the weeks. I am floating. I don't tell him that I keep it because I'm afraid I will need it again.

"Then why do you keep it?"

"I forgot about it," I say. "All that shit they stock in the cabinet. Like I'd remember." I open my eyes enough to see his reaction. He is tossing the bottle back and forth in his hands.

He looks down at my nakedness as if he just noticed it. I look at the tree outside the window, blazing with leaves, as if it is growing out of Ethan's head. "Can you get up and put on some clothes? What if your parents walk in?"

I sit up. I want to pull him inside me, to feel how I shake inside from anger. He tosses my bottle of pills in the kitchen trash. Later, when he sleeps, I dig through orange peels and spaghetti. I wipe tomato sauce off the cap, and roll the bottle between my palms. I think of dumping Ethan. I press the bottle to my lips and change my mind.

On the day of my test, I wait in line to register my name behind an endless string of pimply adolescent boys who have been itching since birth for this day. Their fathers wait in plastic chairs by the windows so they can watch their kids take the test. So if they screw up, they can start screaming, like the guy now, who is walking out to the family car with his son. *We went over parallel parking a hundred goddamn times.* He smacks the kid on his coat sleeve and shoves him out the door. I am excited, thinking of the look on my father's face when I tell him that I got my license, without his help.

Dave is waiting in the parking lot. I told him not to watch me because it would just make me nervous. The woman behind the desk asks for my form, and I hand it back to her and she writes something on it and hands it back to me and I wait.

What do people think of right before they die? I asked my father this last night, as we sat on the porch, drinking beer.

"I don't know," he said. "You probably don't think about anything. You probably die before anything is thought. How the hell should I know? I don't like to think about it."

"You're probably right," I said." I don't like to think about it either. That's why I'm in therapy."

He either didn't think this was funny, or he didn't understand.

Instead, we sipped beers. We counted cars driving on the road paved as shiny as black licorice. Twelve blue ones drove past, thirteen red ones, almost all of them American. Then the sun started to set, and I downed the rest of my beer. I patted my father's head before I went into the house. Later, I lay in the dark, the sounds of cars interrupting my sleep. The thud of doors that don't-quite-close in my dreams.

The state cop has tired eyes. He pushes his glasses up the bridge of his nose. He is bored.

"Now first," he yawns. "I want you to park between those two cones."

I squeeze my eyes shut, then open them, then begin the wheel turning. I crank the wheel too soon and bump the second cone. I look at the cop, and for some reason, I think of my Prozac in the bathroom cabinet, the empty beer cans from my father and me to be re-cycled. I think of Ethan, and how he didn't even call last night to wish me luck on this fucking test.

I'm beginning to doubt my parallel parking abili-ties. The state cop looks worried.

"Young lady, just relax. Try it again."

"You mean, start over?"

He waves his hand as if he's erasing my mistake.

"Yes, yes. Start over. Just pull the car out and try again."

I look ahead to see Dave leaning against the driving center building. I imagine him at sixteen, his face clear of scar and worry. His mother waiting patiently on the side of the driving course, his father waiting angrily at home. I wave to him, but thank God he doesn't see me. I put the car in drive and try again.

I pull out of the space after my second parallel parking attempt. I glance over at the cop for approval. *It'll do*, he says. He directs me to go left onto the road. I see Dave watching from his post at the curb, waving in the rain.

When I am finished with this test, I will go home and call my sister. Pack my suitcase and sit on top of it, a map of Florida balanced on my knees. I will trace in yellow highlighter all the tiny paths that I want to follow. Roads winding south, dropping into the sea. It is a beautiful day for a drive.

My keys jingle in the ignition. I press the pedal and move up to the light. I wait for the light to turn green. I go.

The New Yinzer is a literary organization dedicated to enriching the literary landscape of Western Pennsylvania and beyond by exposing its residents to new and experimental forms of writing not found in other local fora and engaging them in an educational discourse about that writing, while also providing regional writers with a working classroom in which to cultivate their writing from a fresh idea to a finished product.

The New Yinzer first published online on January 30, 2002, and was incorporated as a non-profit company on June 14, 2002.